SPIRIT MAN JINN

AHMED HULUSI

www.ahmedhulusi.org/en/

As with all my works, this book is not copyrighted.
As long as it remains faithful to the original,
it may be freely printed, reproduced, published and translated.
For the knowledge of ALLAH, there is no recompense.

SPIRIT MAN JINN

AHMED HULUSI

www.ahmedhulusi.org/en/

Translated by ALIYA ATALAY

TRANSLATOR'S PREFACE

Throughout the ages, mankind has always been somewhat intimidated yet at the same time enthralled and mystified by the 'unknown', 'unseen' and the 'unidentified' beings: Ghosts, spirits, fairies, demons, entities, aliens, the reptilians… and so on.

Needless to say, they have always been topics of great confusion and controversy. Though their labels, masks and costumes changed every century, the play was always the same; to charm, captivate, spellbind, and eventually dominate their audience: the humans.

Not surprisingly the humans have been falling prey to this conjuring, otherworldly show simply because of their lack of knowledge, caught unawares in the dark theatre of ignorance.

Thankfully these shape-shifting, mind boggling, hoodwinking creatures are no longer an inscrutable enigma. With this book Ahmed Hulusi is literally turning on the flashlights to reveal the true face of these beings.

Although Spirit Man Jinn (*Ruh İnsan Cin*) was originally written in 1971, I believe it is still the most powerful source of information in its field as it not only elucidates this topic in the religious context but also demystifies this phenomenon through the lens of science.

I strongly feel that this book will be of much interest and advantage to the increasing number of people who are directly or indirectly aggrieved by these energies and who are seeking answers and solutions to their disconcerting dilemma.

ALIYA ATALAY
15 March 2022
Istanbul

CONTENTS

PREFACE

One of my favorite quotes from **Mawlana Jalaladdin al-Rumi** is:

"What pertains to the past is left in the past my love;

Now, it is the time to say new things!"

Indeed, **Ahmed Hulusi** is not fond of repeating things from the past!

It goes against his principles to repeat things to which people have gained immunity or resistance and thus can no longer evaluate!

Ahmed Hulusi is not a hodja!

Ahmed Hulusi is not a **sheikh**!

Ahmed Hulusi is not **religious leader**!

Through **"divine warning"** he began to objectively research the reality of **"religion."**

Starting with the hadith collection **"Qutub al-Sittah"** he has researched and applied all the requisites of **Sufism** including all its fine intricacies, **then decoded the religious metaphors based on modern scientific knowledge to bring about the synthesis needed for our present day.**

According to **Ahmed Hulusi "Religion, is a holistic SYSTEM"**!

This system, may be easily understood by any level of intellect that is interested in it, as neither the **Quran** nor the hadiths have left any topic unexplained…

The important thing is to correctly decipher the codes!

So, then what is incumbent on an intellectual is to discover and make the most of this invaluable treasure of knowledge that has been granted to him!

You will find my explanations and interpretations in this book and all future books to be more **scientifically advanced and aligned to the modern age, perhaps even surpassing this age...**

Allah willing, you will benefit from these ideas and perspectives that are of a quality to bring about not a reform in religion, but a new religious UNDERSTANDING.

I pray that this book will be beneficial to all of humanity, and wish conscious and 'jinn-free' days to all of you!

AHMED HULUSI

21.1.1990

Antalya

1

INTRODUCTION

Since the first publication of this book in 1972 I have been endowed with many blessings in regards to the secrets and mysteries of the system of creation.

Some of them I penned in "The Human Enigma" (1986) and some in "Muhammad's Allah" (1989) …

However, I chose to leave some of the relevant topics to this book…

I tried to share in this publication comprehensive information and extensive details on the topics of "Spirit", "Aliens", "Angels," and the afterlife make-up of "Man" compared to previous works…

I'd like to first provide some introductory information on the jinn and the aliens, the existence of which, sadly, many primitive brains refuse to accept, even at the expense of denying the Quran …

There is a great misconception that most of us have regarding the jinn…

Some of us think…

The jinn are short stout beings of around 70-90 cm height with crossed legs, long ears and cat eyes, and who are fast moving shapeshifters…

And some of us think…

The jinn are pure hallucinations that people with certain brain disorders have...

So, what's the truth of the matter?

Let us first know with certainty that a person is either a megalomaniac, paranoid, schizophrenic who thinks they know "everything" or they are mature enough to admit that besides what they have read and know, there are still much that they do not know…

Denial is from primitiveness, while knowing one's place is from wisdom and perfection…

There are so many individuals who deny the truth out of ignorance and then end up accepting it when they encounter new information!

Let us take heed from all of this…!

Let us know that...

Our biggest mistake is to think of aliens as physical material beings like ourselves…!

Our second biggest downfall is our addiction to our preconditioned ideas and hence our inability to re-evaluate the meanings anew, thereby getting blocked and stuck on the surface value and literal meanings of words.

For example, when we hear the word "jinn" our first reaction is to deny it and say, "There can't be such things; it's absurd, it's made-up!"

Whereas if we do the research perhaps, we're going to learn so many new things and find the answers to so many of our questions…

Now let us, despite the blockage in our brain, try to contemplate objectively, comprehensively and without prejudice…and take the human body for example…

We know the human body is comprised of trillions of cells… The vital force that controls the functioning of this body is bioelectrical energy…

Brain activity takes place solely with bioelectrical energy…

Because in the past 'bioelectrical energy' wasn't known, symbolic and metaphoric language was used to describe it.

The classical religious understanding states that there is an inanimate physical body and also a spirit that enters this body and gives life to it, and that consciousness comes from this spirit…

This isn't the case!

Life is present in every iota of the universe!

Life is consciousness and consciousness is life!

Hence there is nothing not alive or unconscious in the universe!

However, let us not overlook an important point…

Since our brains are restricted with the five senses and hence our thoughts are blocked, it is normal that we don't accept the existence of other 'more' conscious beings than ourselves in the universe!

The brain only takes into account the data it can perceive through the five senses, anything outside the scope of these senses it disregards, just like animals…

Whereas a brain that is limited by the five senses can neither understand television waves, nor radar waves, nor any other scientifically verified phenomenon whose visibility falls outside the spectrum of our sight…

Let us know…

The five senses have been given to us so that we may take little snippets of examples from the WHOLE EXISTENCE…

Yet we have fallen into a great mistake, instead of using our senses to try to understand and evaluate the WHOLE, we have on the contrary become blocked and restricted by them and then reduced and confined everything to what we perceive through them…

From beings that are the size of a trillionth of a centimeter to those comprised of wavelengths that are the distance of kilometers, the universe is full of conscious beings, what we perceive among them is not even a drop compared to the ocean…

This being the case, it is such great primitiveness and ignorance to claim, "everything is confined to what I perceive through my senses, what I don't perceive does not exist" …

The molecular structures that compose the super atomic dimensions, and all the waves that comprise the subatomic dimensions comprise only a part of the scale of "conscious beings" in the universe…

All beings that compose the subatomic dimensions are referred to as "angels" in religious literature…

Essentially all beings are categorized into two groups in the divine sources…

"Angels" and "Humans & Jinn" …

From the level of the atoms to that of pure energy, all quantum based radial beings are called "angels" and all those that are above this level are referred to as "humans and jinn" …

The word "jinn" also known as the aliens, exist in the form of waves, they have a holographic make-up…

Similarly, the spirit of man, is also a holographic wave body made of brain waves.

Just as an organ in the human body, say the liver, consciously and deliberately functions in a particular way, and also works inter-dependently yet in unison with all the other organs forming the body and human consciousness…

In the same way there are sub-atomic and super-atomic dimensions comprised of systemic, galactic conscious beings that in religious terms are referred to as angels.

Everything in existence derives its life and consciousness from angels…

Just like the atoms and subatomic levels comprising the structure of a 'computer' involve a dimensional depth, an essence... in the same way, the essence comprising a human, an animal, or a jinn, is called an angel…

Thus, the essence of all humans, jinn, and animals are angelic forces…

The reason why the jinn are often confused with the angels and why the Satan is thought to be an angel of high rank is because people don't understand this distinction very well…

The misconception that "Iblis" - who is angelic by essence but a jinn by make-up and compositional structure - is generally known as an "archangel" is also based on this…

The Quran elucidates this truth with the verse:

"And when We said to the angels, 'Prostrate to Adam,' and all but Iblis prostrated. He was of the jinn..."[1]

The jinn habitually do not 'prostrate' i.e., accept the superiority of and submit to, mankind!

And they won't!

For, the qualities of their make-up surpass those of humans!

---

[1] Quran 18:50

The angels, not only compose the essence of all animate and inanimate beings, they also exist as conscious beings in various sizes and dimensions...

It is a great wonder to people how the angels administer over mankind...

Let's take for example Azrael, the angel of death... People ask, is Azrael one or many, how can he kill so many people all at the same time?

Let me explain with a simple example...

A space craft is sent to Uranus and controlled via radio waves sent from NASA centers and facilities to fulfill specific functions... There are many such satellites in our orbit all of which are controlled and administered with the radio waves from NASA centers...

Similarly, the angel Azrael sends specific waves to deactivate specific circuitry in the brain, shutting down its function and hence fulfilling the phenomenon we call death...

Just as NASA can administer countless space crafts from a single center, Azrael can also send certain waves to countless brains at the same time to fulfill his task.

In the same way all of the angels broadcast specific waves to brains, or in more philosophical terms, they administer mankind by affecting their genetic code and the "radial wave body" we call the "spirit" ...

There are angels that don't have a defined form and exist only as pure consciousness, as well as angels that do have form, according to the intimates of the reality...

Just as the human body has a spirit, the stars and constellations also have a spirit, also referred to as angelic beings in religious texts...

Additionally, every planet and star, including the Sun, has its own inhabitants, which are also considered to be angels...

The inhabitants of the Sun for example, are called "*Zabani*" in religious literature. They've been named this according to the people who will go there... *Zabani* means to make *zabun,* which means to despise, disdain, scorn and look down upon...

They are not evil by nature, however extremely resilient due to the conditions of the Sun in which they live, and have the ability to move remarkably fast compared to us...

Because human spirits are accustomed to the weaker gravitational force of the Earth, when they get stuck inside the Sun their strength will be severely inadequate; they will be weak and vulnerable there...

Some hadith say the body will be exceedingly large in the Sun and those who go there will only be able to crawl and creep their way through as their bodies will be too large and heavy to move. All of this validate the expected difficulty of the transition from the very low gravitational pull of the Earth to the immensely high gravitational force of the Sun...

The jinn who go to the Sun, i.e., 'hell', will also be prone to suffering and tortured by its inhabitants as they too will not be able to adapt to the formidable conditions of the Sun.

All planets and stars, like the Sun, have inhabitants that are specific to them, and this is natural and necessary...

But because we suspect that all beings are made of flesh and bones like ourselves and expect them to be visible to the human eye, we squander away our lives in a vicious and unproductive cycle...

With this introductory information, let us now move on to the main topic of spirit, man, jinn and the aliens...

AHMED HULUSI
Antalya - 1990

2

BEWARE!

I'd like to first touch on the topics of necromancy and alien contact, which is becoming more and more popular by the day...

What started as "alleged communication with the dead" and eventually evolved into "making contact with aliens" is nothing other than the deception and hoax of the jinn!

Those who are interested in such things clearly do not heed the warnings of neither Muhammad (saw) nor the Quran...

They construe and interpret the verses of the Quran as they like and deny many along the way...

The truth is, all of the scholars are of the same opinion regarding this topic.

The Quran is a holistic source; one either accepts it completely or denies it completely. To deny a single verse is the same as denying the entire thing.

Unfortunately, however, while some construe the verses according to their vested interests, some deny them altogether.

Here are some verses from the Quran showing the impossibility of returning to the world after death:

> **When death comes to one of them, he says, "My Rabb, send me back** (to the worldly life).**"**
>
> **"So that I might do righteousness in that which I left behind** (i.e. a faithful life that I did not heed or give importance to; the potential

that I did not utilize and activate).**" No!** (It is impossible to go back!) **His words are invalid!** (His request is unrecognized in the system) **and behind them is a barrier** (an isthmus; a difference of dimension) **until the Day they are resurrected** (they cannot go back; reincarnation, being re-born for another worldly life, is not possible!).

So, when the Horn is blown (when the process of resurrection, i.e. a new beginning commences), **no relationship** (worldly interactions, family relations, titles or familiar faces) **will there be among them that Day, nor will they ask about one another** (in terms of earthly relations).[2]

Besides these there are many verses stating things like:

"They will say, 'Send us back to the world so that we may do the things we didn't do', but after death they can never go back to the world…"

The biggest deception of the alleged "spirits" and "aliens" is this idea they inject into man; that he can come back to the world after death. One who believes this has refused the religion of Islam…

For, the Quran and Muhammad (saw) has made it very clear that until the day all humans are resurrected collectively (Doomsday - *bath'u ba'dal mawt*) and given new bodies they can never come back to this dimension of life…This is one of the pillars of faith.

The Quran says the following regarding the beings known as "the jinn":

"O community of jinn, you have truly possessed (misled from reality) **the vast majority of mankind."**[3]

This verse shows that the "majority" of mankind is either consciously or unconsciously under the effect of the jinn and are hence misled from the reality… The verse continues as such:

---

[2] Quran 23: 99-101
[3] Quran 6:128

And their allies among mankind will say, "Our Rabb, we mutually benefited from each other, and we have now reached our term, which you appointed for us." He will say, "The Fire is your residence, wherein you will abide eternally, except for what Allah wills..." Indeed, your Rabb is the *Hakim* and the *Aleem*.[4]

How do the jinn cause deception and delusion to the majority of humans?

They spread misinformation regarding the future events by distorting the information relayed by the Nabis and Rasuls...

Hence the people who have been wrongly guided, unaware of what is awaiting them, do not take the precautions they need to take in order to be prepared! They take the wrong route, go after the wrong purpose, and when they realize the truth alas, it is way too late!

Let us always be mindful of the following:

1. The jinn, like humans, exists as colonies and families, but their population far outweighs that of humans... there are trillions and trillions of jinn...

2. They have a wave based, holographic radial body... They can easily send signals to the human brain to incite specific thoughts, manipulate thought patterns, cause illusion and delusion, and make them see things that don't really exist, hence causing great provocation...

3. They have the ability to burn through matter with rays, and some can even carry an object from any point of the Earth to another...

4. Those who refuse the religion of Islam accept various philosophical views as though they are new.

5. You can't find a single person who knows and accepts the Islamic way and believes in making contact with spirits through psychics.

6. The Westerners who believe in the spirits do not know about the jinn! Christianity does not talk about the jinn. Hence what we call the jinn,

---

[4] Quran 6:128

they call spirits, entities, ghosts, Satan etc... All of these are nothing other than different names for the jinn.

7. According to those who make contact with spirits and aliens Muhammad (saw) is simply a psychic! Again, this is a misleading idea generated by the jinn.

8. There are many men and women today who lack Islamic knowledge, who are possessed by the jinn and who sadly believe they are saints.

9. The jinn can access knowledge of the past and narrate this information through whoever they like... Hence one who can give information from the past or can suddenly speak a new language in a state of "trance" is not because their spirits have lived in the past; it is the jinn talking through them.

Let me try to answer some common questions:

If one consciously or unconsciously becomes possessed by the jinn how can they overcome this situation? What can they do to take precaution and protection?

My advice is:

1. The following verses have a profound effect on neutralizing and removing the effects of the jinn:

Chapter Saad Verse 41,

Chapter al-Mu'minun Verses 97-98,

Chapter as-Saffat Verse 7.

As precaution and protection for those who are involved in Sufism, I recommend the recital of these verses 40 times every morning and evening.

Those who've been affected by the jinn should recite these verses at least 100-300 times every morning and evening, they will see the results in a short period of time...

Here is the transliteration and translation of these verses:

"Rabbi inni massaniyash shaytanu Bi noosbin wa adhab; Rabbi audhu bika min hamazatish shayateen wa audhu bika Rabbi an yahdhuroon. Wa hıfzan min qulli shaytanin mareed."

"O Rabb! (The Reality of the Names comprising my essence) Satan (The internal mechanism (ego) that promotes the illusory existence of the inexistent and veils the absolute reality) is distressing and tormenting me. My Rabb, I seek refuge in you from the incitements of Satan, and I seek refuge in you from the presence of Satanic influences around me. And protected it from every rebellious Satan."[5]

2. Those who are strongly affected by the jinn, who think they've seen them or had alien contact, should recite the following prayer 1000 times every day for 40 days consecutively:

Audhu bi wajhillahil kareem wa kalimatillahil ta'ammatilladhiy la yujawuz hunna barrun wala fajiroon min sharri ma yanzilu minas samaa'i wa ma ya'rujoo feeyha wa min sharri ma zara'a fil ardhi wa mayakhrujoo minha wa min fitanil layli wan nahari illa tariqan yatruku bikhayrin ya Rahman...

I seek refuge in the face of Allah (in that which the attributes of Allah become manifest), the Karim (The exceedingly generous and bountiful), and in all His Names, nothing good or bad can attack them.

I seek protection in RAHMAN, the source of all potentials, from that which ascends to the heavens (from provocative thoughts) and that which descends from the heavens (from thoughts that conjure doubt and suspicion), from that which is produced from the plane of perceived manifestation (ardh) (that which emanates from corporeality) and grows out of it (bodily demands and desires), from the provocations of the day (our internal life) and the night (the outside world), and from that which knocks on the door at night (instinct), except if it is with good intent.

---

[5] Quran 38:41, 23:97-98, 37: 7

ɔ. Recite chapter 113-114 (Al-falaq - An-nas) 41 times per day.

4. Recite the prayer: **La hawle wala quwwata illa Billahil aliyyul azim** 100-500 times per day.

Finally, I'd like to stress the point that all adversities that come upon man are due to his ignorance. The most common and immediate defense that is made is "But that's what I THOUGHT, that's what I HEARD!"

Don't squander your life with what you hear and assume to be true, do the research, find the truth, base your life on facts not assumptions, if you don't want to be in eternal remorse in the afterlife that is!

Thousands of people die every day and move on to a realm in which they no longer can do anything that can benefit them...

We have a whole eternity at stake my friends! It is a matter of urgency!

The first thing we have to save is our future! Life after death is very different to what we think or know!

Let us be among the people of knowledge! Let us acquire our knowledge from the actual sources, not from other people! Let us be prepared and not be in eternal regret after we die!

If you believe there is life after death;

Take a look at how much of your day you're spending in the way of worldly matters, for things that you're going to leave behind when you die, and how much of your day you're spending engaging in practices that are going to benefit you in your eternal afterlife?

Does your answer make you happy?

If it doesn't turn to knowledge and search for the truth!

Don't gamble with your eternal life! Its compensation is impossible!

May your day and night be filled with beneficial knowledge.

AHMED HULUSI
7.3.1989
Antalya

3

RELIGION AND SCIENCE

On one hand we have loads of religious information passed on throughout the centuries, on the other hand we have the world of science overturning everything we thought we knew…

Many people today totally disregard religious information as "outdated" because it came 1400 years ago and used a language that addressed the people of that time. Due to this it is either misunderstood, or not understood at all in modern times. The failure to decode the metaphors and symbolic language of religion has turned many people away from the "Book" and the "Call" leading them to consider it as "superstitious nonsense" …

On the other hand, science has made tremendous advances, especially in the last century, and has turned everything we know upside down…

Many scientists such as Albert Einstein, Max Planck, Louis De Broglie, Schrodinger, Davisson and Germer have presented theories that have literally reconstructed the mental world of modern man…

The current scientific view asserts that:

a. The building block of matter is a single element; hydrogen,

b. A star turns matter into energy by the process of **nuclear fusion,**

c. The universe is a gigantic electromagnetic field,

d. Matter can change form with speed; at high speeds it can turn into energy and surpass the state of matter,

e. Electrodynamics reflect the truth more accurately than mechanics,

f. Time and space are relative,

g. Energy has mass,

h. The basic unit of all light is a photon.

These and many other such phenomenon that were not known in the past are now accepted by science, while poor Galileo was tried by the Inquisition and put through excruciating torture just because he said the Earth revolves around the Sun…

I want to now draw your attention to an important point before I move on…

All scientists are in unison today with the idea that the 'stability' of all forms of matter, whether solid or liquid exists only in appearance; in reality matter is made of atoms that are in *constant motion*…

In light of modern science, many intellectuals state that it is our crude and coarse nature that prevents us from perceiving the atomic make-up of matter…

They also claim that the universe is made of electromagnetic waves, and that it is a holistic form beyond human cognition…

That is, the understanding that "everything is matter, there is nothing beyond matter" which was widely accepted until recently has now become totally depleted, and in its stead a new vision, that of a 'boundless universe' has emerged…

Humans who live on Earth with their five senses – a point where these waves "densify" so to speak, have deciphered a deep secret and moved beyond matter, so to speak, through their ability to contemplate…

How did this seemingly material man discover such a truth with such limited senses?

Let us explore this step by step…

For the first time William Prout, an English chemist and physician, hypothesized that every atom that makes up an object is comprised of hydrogen atoms and hence the hydrogen atom is the only truly fundamental particle in the make-up of the universe.

In 1911 in Langevin he proved that 16 hydrogen atoms make up one oxygen atom and thus the universe is essentially made of multiples of a single element.

This validated the principle of the "unity of existence" asserted by religious teachings...

After this Albert Einstein said:

"Matter is energy and energy is matter! The difference between them is in passing... If matter becomes sparse and its speed increases to dramatically, we call it radiation or energy... If on the other hand it becomes dense and heavy whereby, we can calculate its mass, we call it 'matter'..."

As a matter of fact, for the first time in July 1945 in New Mexico a part of matter was converted to light, motion, sound and energy...

After that the notion of the electron, which was assumed to be round, changed to 'electrical charge' and the conception of the atom changed to 'stacks of waves' rather than a 'particle'...

In short it has become evident that all of matter consists of frequencies, waves and that we are in effect living in a universe of waves...

These are the observations of scientists...

But *we* too can analyze the realm of waves!

Let us consider some examples of waves and rays that can be determined with the senses...

1. The sound waves perceived by dogs,
2. The sound waves perceived by humans,
3. The sound waves perceived by cats,
4. Ultrasonic waves,
5. Radio waves (L – long, M – medium, S – short waves that are converted by an adaptor called a radio),
6. Television waves (VHF, UHF, SHF, EHF – all of which are converted by an adaptor called a television),
7. Radar waves,
8. Spark waves,
9. Motion waves,
10. The spectrum of rays that we see as colors between red and purple, perceived by our eyes...

11. Ultraviolet rays,
12. X-rays,
13. Cosmic rays (of wavelength shorter than 1/10,000000000000 of a cm),
14. And various other "unidentified" rays…

There are many more however we humans do not know their nature and effects as yet...

Because the crude and limited nature of the human senses are unable to perceive and understand the innumerous rays present in the universe unfortunately, they are mostly regarded as non-existent…

But is this true?

The difference between seeing and not seeing lies within the range of 1-3/100,000 of a cm…

The point at which the human eye begins to perceive is 0,0004 cm, where the ultraviolet rays begin, and ends at 0,0007 cm where infrared rays begin… it is an extremely narrow spectrum!

Whereas the Sun permeates many different rays that begin at 0,0008 cm and reach 0,032 cm……

Much shorter rays can be detected by film…

There are ultraviolet rays that range between 0,0003 cm and 0,0001 cm, and even shorter, but these can only be determined via photograph plates.

Let us look into the X-rays a little further:

We all know that when our bodies are exposed to X-rays the energy that is produced is directed towards a metal plate to reveal certain parts of our organs.

We also know that this radiation that beams through the body is harmful and causes some damage to the organs, and hence pregnant women or new born babies are not advised to get an x-ray.

On the other hand, while these rays are beamed through our body *we don't feel or perceive them*… their wavelength is about 1/100,000000 of a cm…

So, I ask you:

While man cannot detect or feel these x-rays whose wavelengths are inexplicably small with his senses, how can we deny the existence of those with much higher frequencies?

How can we deny the existence of beings whose make-up comprises similar waves or frequencies just because we can't perceive them?

The make-up of the beings Islam refers to as "jinn" – what most people know as spirits or entities- is described in the following verse:

"Min MARIJINN min NAR"[6] which means "smokeless flame of fire" (radiation, radiant energy, electromagnetic wave body).

And "Min NAARis SAMUM"[7] which means **'samum' fire** (an infusing, penetrating microwave radiation that is harmful to the astral body)."

A fire that is:

SMOKELESS

TOXIC

PENETRATING...

is precisely what we today call "radiation"!

1400 years ago, the radial make-up of the jinn was described as a smokeless, toxic, infusing FIRE...

This is one of the biggest miracles of the Quran in my opinion... to describe that we know as rays and radiation as a smokeless, harmful fire that penetrates through the skin!

Based on this description then the make-up of the jinn is;

A smokeless fire -that we know as waves today- that can penetrate into all layers of matter"

---

[6] Quran 55:15
[7] Quran 15:27

Clearly, we can't expect the Quran to have said 1400 years ago "We created the jinn from radiation waves of such and such type"! It is evident that to bring this concept closer to human cognition "1400 years ago" without using the word "radiation" – a word that did not exist at the time - the Quran had to use a metaphor and describe it as a "smokeless harmful fire" that can "penetrate into all layers of the skin".

Thankfully after 1400 years science has advanced enough to discover rays and radiation waves, at least to some extent, and hence enabled those who can bridge religion with science to decode the realities referenced by these symbolic verses, allowing us to have a better, more scientific understanding of the nature of these beings called the "jinn" …

After this short introduction, let us now turn back to the world of science and review the realities underlying the terms "Spirit", "Man" and "Jinn" …

4

A UNIVERSE OF WAVES AND THE ILLUSION OF MULTIPLICITY

There was a young man in the Swiss Patent Office in Bern, he was only 26 years old… They used to call him Albert but in time, his way of thinking made him reach global fame and soon after people started calling him: "Einstein" …

The first thing Einstein did was to publish a report that shifted the world of science to a brand-new field of physics… the year was 1905…

His first theory totally transformed our concept on time and space…

Regarding space Einstein asserted that, time and space are intertwined into a single continuum known as space-time, that space is merely an order of possibilities, events that occur at the same time for one observer could occur at different times for another, and that time is not external, but something we experience in our minds.

He said, "Concerning matter, we have been all wrong. What we have called matter is energy, whose vibration has dropped enough to be perceptible to the senses. There is no matter."

Einstein more openly claimed, "Space is not a separate external phenomenon… It was formerly believed that if all material things disappeared out of the universe, time and space would be left. According to relativity theory, however, time and space disappear together with the things. They are not independent of one another."

As science was rapidly advancing, in 1915, Langevin proved that everything perceived as matter in the universe was made of a single element. Again, thanks to the previous theories presented by Einstein.

Meanwhile, around 1900, Max Planck had also presented a theory and had answered a question that couldn't be answered for a long time…

Physicists had trouble explaining the way in which hot bodies radiate energy. If a red-hot nail is heated even more, its light will be orange, then yellow, green, blue and violet. This meant there were energy radiation of differing wavelengths, depending on the intensity of the heat. Which formula or law did this observation fit in with?

Max Planck answered:

"Radiation is not a steady stream of energy, but rather energy is radiated and absorbed in small indivisible portions, which are called *quanta…*"

Planck's claim was not understood until Einstein's theory of special relativity.

Based on this Albert Einstein determined that light exists in discrete quanta of energy, or photons, where photons: **behave both like a particle and a wave**. … they can have particle-like interactions (i.e. collisions) with electrons and other particles, such as in the Compton effect in which particles of light collide with atoms, causing the release of electrons.

He inferred, "Ultraviolet radiation has shorter waves than blue or violet light, and thus oscillates more rapidly and carries more energy, and that the speed of an electron that is ejected when light strikes the plate in an evacuated tube, is equal to the energy carried by the photons that strike it."

Einstein received a Nobel prize **for this discovery which was called the law of the photoelectric effect.**

Later, Einstein published an article deducing that electromagnetic radiation itself consists of "particles" of energy, but the overwhelming evidence of the "wave" nature of this radiation was more widely accepted by his peers, and for some time the true nature of energy remained a mystery…

Finally in 1925, Louis De Broglie proposed that any object has wavelike properties, not just light, and that the wave nature of energy was more realistic than particle…

Meanwhile it was seen that electrons were not tiny solid spheres that can be observed and measured and that in fact their exact position and momentum could be determined.

Then **Sir J. Jeans** shared his thought:

"A solid spherical object has a specific location in space, its position can be determined, it also has mass… However, this is not the case with an electron… Just as trying to determine the position and mass of a certain fear or curiosity which emerges in one's heart is absurd, the same applies to electrons…"

In 1927 Austrian physicist Erwin Schrödinger published papers that established the foundation of quantum mechanics.

In the same year two American scientists Davisson and Germer demonstrated and proved the wave-nature of electrons and thus the truth of matter started to fall into place…

The electron, which was assumed to be a tiny solid sphere in the past, changed to 'electrical charge' and the conception of the atom changed to 'stacks of waves' rather than a 'particle' leading us to accept the truth that matter consists of frequencies, waves and that we are in effect living in a universe of waves…

But Einstein didn't stop there…

He said matter and energy are interchangeable, and hence matter can be transformed into energy…

He explained that the mass of a moving object increases with speed and eventually turns into energy, which means the mass of a moving object increases. In other words, he said energy equals mass multiplied by the square of the speed of light ($E = mc2$).

This means, if one kg of coal can be turned into energy, 25 billion kilowatt-hours of electricity can be obtained – which the US can only produce in two months using all its energy sources!

After all of this, one very important question still remains unanswered…

"What is the essence and origin of this mass or energy? Where does it come from? Where does the power it carries come from?"

Another question is:

If matter can be transformed into energy, can energy be transformed back to matter? Is this possible?

Objective science was able to change matter into energy! But we still don't know if that energy can be changed back into its original 'material' state...

I believe that just as matter can be changed into energy, sooner or later science is going to discover a way of reverting that energy back into its original state, i.e. back to matter...

In Sufism, Islam mysticism, this phenomenon is explained as "tayyi maqan" or "teleportation" which is also what the event known as "Isra" (Ascension) in the Quran is about...

Just as clairvoyance is now openly and publicly broadcast, I believe teleportation will also become just as common...

A saint of our times said:

"If we couldn't observe Egypt from our mat, you couldn't see Europe from here..." i.e. If this potential didn't exist in the human brain and make-up, you wouldn't be able to discover and invent the TV.

Everything that science proves and verifies is the natural state that a Sufi lives in his normal daily life... [8]

Resultantly, the objective scientific boundary of man today is defined externally by "relativity" and internally by "quantum" physics...

While relativity objectively constructs our perception of time, space, gravity, and the realities of size and distance beyond our capacity to comprehend...

Quantum physics has forced us to accept the realities beyond comprehension regarding matter, atoms, energy units and their attributes...

---

[8] More detail can be found on this topic in *The Human Enigma* and *The Observing One*.

24

While in the past scientists used to think everything consists of matter and nothing beyond matter exists, today someone who denies the realities beyond perceivable matter is considered simple and primitive!

A century ago, physicists considered the 'redness' of a rose a 'subjective' quality and considered 'red' to be the vibration of space...

Today physicists claim the color red is a wavelength and accept that it is an energy that consists of photons...

Based on all of this, a well-known physicist has mockingly said:

"Man should adopt the quantum way on Mondays, Wednesdays, and Fridays, and the wave mechanics way on Tuesdays, Thursdays and Saturdays!"

Eventually, both are essentially subjective concepts produced by the imagination...

Concepts such as gravity, electromagnetic energy, momentum, atom, photon are eventually born from an idea, they are 'assumed' into existence for the purpose of finding the truth of what is really out there... They are man-made concepts...

All of the information I shared above, the amazing advancement of science, has shown a single reality to mankind, and forced us to accept it:

Other than the known material world there is an amazing unknown world beyond our comprehension...

One who denies this meta-physical world, this immaterial dimension, displays his primitiveness, oblivious of whether he lives at the end of the 21st century or at within the depths of the world of science...

Such denial, is in fact, a defense mechanism, to cover one's ignorance!

After this little detour into the world of science, let us return to our main topic:

Let us, within this vast universe of various electromagnetic waves, try to understand the reality of man, spirit and jinn…

Do beings with whom 'contact' is made, really exist? If so, what are they?

After extensive research I did to write this book in 1972, I can say with certainty that yes, indeed such beings do exist! You will find detailed information in the coming chapters to prove this, however there are a few important points I'd like to touch on here.

As we know, humans perceive the world through their five senses. Hence the universe perceived by man is different to the universe perceived by another creature, say an animal, who has different perceptive capacity. Here is a simple example:

The human eye perceives waves between 4000-7000 angstrom and sends these to the brain. The brain decodes these waves into an image. Based on this we conclude that these things exist, and those outside this range don't exist.

This is indeed where we go wrong! Even though we can only perceive a tiny section of an endless infinite range of waves, we think existence consists only of what we see within this microscopic range and disregard everything else!

The universe consists of infinite waves or 'quants'.. what we perceive of this endless ocean of waves is not even a single drop!

Secondly:

Since the waves between 4000-7000 angstrom that reach our brain through our eyes and the sound waves between 16-16000 hertz that we hear carry a meaning, then the entire universe with ALL of its wavelengths also carries a meaning of HOLISTIC INTEGRALITY! Yet sadly we are deprived of evaluating this universal holism due to the limitations of our senses.

Our conditioned and restricted perception prevents us from recognizing the ONENESS disguised as many!

Additionally, our limited five sensed perception makes us delusively disregard the existence of infinite forms of life outside our extremely

narrow range, making us stuck within primitive notions and conceptions.

We know scientifically that if we were able to perceive at the atomic level, we would have perceived everything homogeneously and holistically as a single existence.

For example, if you had an enormous electron microscope that magnified your living room a billion times, all you would see are the atoms in your room, a homogeneous mass of elements made of iron, copper, zinc, oxygen, hydrogen, nitrogen, etc…

You will no longer see separate objects that you call a chair or a table that you see when you look with your eyes…!

Hence, what you see and perceive change dramatically depending on your vantage point and the capacity of your perceptive ability… What you see and perceive in the universe are fictitious things projected from the tool you use to perceive it!

So everything we humans see, are merely the projections of our brains, i.e. they are **according** to the perception capacity of the brain; they are limited and constricted projections based on an extremely limited data…

Where does this take us?

When you journey toward your essence through the layers of matter – cell – molecule – atom – neutron – neutrino – quark – and into the depths of the the quantum level you come to such a UNIFIED FIELD, such ONENESS that nothing other than this ONE remains.

This "Cosmic Consciousness" or "Universal Energy", this SINGULAR make-up that we call the universe executes its own system at every instance not bound by time or space.

So, what is our place, who are we and our associates within this ONENESS?

Since we are never really talking about THE universe but OUR universe, is it possible to say there is no other life form out there?

No matter how much technology develops and advances, the human brain confined within the limits of the waves that reach it through its limited capacity, is now helplessly and imperatively admitting that there are countless dimensions and life forms beyond the one it can perceive...

Then, if we think in line with scientific evidence, we can clearly see and accept that outside our seemingly material world there are innumerous forms of life who are also equally material in their own dimension but 'radial' or 'immaterial' ACCORDING to our perception...

Until a few decades ago, the world of science was addicted to a primitive materialist view. Matter was everything, and nothing other than perceivable matter existed... Now, the 'materialist' way of thinking has become extremely outdated and is considered extremely archaic.

Is the universe entirely a radial field of energy but we are living in a material dimension?

This is the most important part to understand!

Is there a material and an immaterial dimension to this universe? Do animate beings live in a material world?

The latest scientific findings show that everything we perceive from the cosmological systems comprising the "macrocosmos" to the muons and quarks composing the "microcosmos" are compositional layers that form one another. Each of these layers are "physical" according to its perceiver!

That is, concepts such as 'physical' or 'material' are entirely **relative** and change according to the capacity of the perceiver.

For those whose perceptive ability score two points higher than ours, our dimension is meta-physical, yet for those who score two points lower our 'physical' dimension doesn't even exist!

While a cell or a bacteria living in our body isn't even aware of our existence, how can we assert there are no other forms of conscious life besides ourselves?

How can we deny the existence of higher levels of matter and their inhabitants?

Whether we take it as waves or quantal make-up, realistic evaluation of the universe brings us to the conclusion that there are countless animate conscious beings besides us!

Unfortunately, however, because we haven't been able to cleanse ourselves from the primitive materialist view of the 19th century, we are unable to make a leap to the realm of the universal realities and values, confining ourselves to the narrow limits of what we perceive as matter.

We must know with certainty that from the quantum dimension to the seemingly material plane we perceive with our senses and the galactic realms, every compositional structure has consciousness and values specific to itself.

To the extent we discern this and deepen our understanding of them we can make contact with these other forms of consciousness. Narrowminded denial spawns nothing other than blinded consciousness.

In conclusion, besides humans, there are most certainly and doubtlessly many other forms of life and consciousness in the universe.

How do those who have overcome the blockage of their senses and who have mounted the wagon of contemplation on the path enlightened by the projector of religion and science understand "spirit" "man" and "jinn"?

Among these we only know "man" in respect of his external make-up…

So let us begin our examination with the "spirit" …

5

WHAT IS THE "SPIRIT"?

Many people, based on hearsay, ask me:

"Even though the Quran does not even provide the Rasul of Allah (saw) with information regarding the spirit, how can you make explanations about the spirit?"

Let us begin with answering this question…

Three Jewish scholars decide to verify the authenticity of the Rasul of Allah (saw) by asking him three questions, one of which is concerning the spirit. Since no previous Rasul has made any explanation regarding the spirit, if Muhammad (saw) does, then we will know he is a hoax, they decide.

So, they ask him, "What is the spirit?"

The Rasul of Allah (saw) answers, "Come back tomorrow, Allah willing, I will answer your question then."

The next day when they come back the Rasul (saw) recites the verse:

"And they (the Jews) **ask you,** (O Muhammad) **about the spirit. Say, "The spirit is from the command** (*amr*; the manifestation of the Names) **of my Rabb. And you (the Jews) have been given little of this knowledge."**[9]

As can be seen this verse directly addresses the Jews who asked the question, not the saints, scholars or the Nabis. This is evident with the

---

[9] Quran 17:85

31

expression, "THEY ask you" and "Say" i.e. tell them, the Jews, that they have been given little of this knowledge.

In other words, this verse is saying:

"The Jews, who think everything is composed of matter, who deny what they cannot perceive through their sensory perception, and who deny the Rasul despite the fact that he tells them the truth, have no knowledge of the spirit! They are bound to live with whatever they've been given because the doors of mysticism and abstract realities have been closed to them as they are not able to perceive anything beyond their senses! This is also why they refused to accept Jesus (pbuh) who explained 'the real world is the world of the spirits'. How then do they expect to be given any knowledge of the spirit?"

As such, Imam Ghazali says in the first volume of his collection "Ihya-u Ulumiddeen":

"Do not assume that the Rasul of Allah (saw) did not know the reality of the Spirit! For, one who knows not his spirit knows not himself! So how then, one who knows not himself, know his Rabb? Just as this knowledge has been disclosed to the Rasuls and the Nabis, it has also been disclosed to some saints and scholars!"

On the topic of **Imam Ghazali** let us not continue without mentioning two of his works in which he shares invaluable knowledge on the reality of the spirit.

The first is "Mishqatul Anwar" (Lantern of Lights) which covers topics like the reality of the spirit, the Oneness of Allah - that nothing exists besides Allah…

The second is, "Kitab'ul maznun bih ala ghayri ahlihi" which also includes sacred information on the spirit. Here is an excerpt:

"Some of the inquirers have asked us to cast a ray of light on the mysteries of the human soul and the meaning of 'taswiyah'…

I told them, when matter is fit enough to attract the soul, and consequently the latter enters the former, this entry is called taswiyah.

That matter is the refined and specially prepared dust in respect of Adam and sperm in respect of his descendants…

Nafh (breath) here means the result of breathing spirit into man so as to activate the light of the spirit in the sperm

In the same way when sperm is stable and moderate, Allah breathes spirit into it, and there is no change in Allah Himself.

What must not be taken for granted is that the **soul comes into existence when the sperm enters the womb…"**

Ghazali continues:

"The spirit is not a state of matter, it is not a substance, it does not penetrate our bodies like water filling the contents of a pot. A substance can be divided, whereas the spirit is indivisible. If it were divisible then this would imply that two spirits could be unequal in cognition, i.e. that it would know and be ignorant at the same time which is ridiculously absurd and contradictory.

The human spirit is indivisible - to call it a part is fallacious, since a part belongs to the whole, and here there is no whole and no part. The human spirit is indivisible and it does not occupy space.

The human spirit is not pre-eternal; it is created when matter is fit to receive it. Hence it is a creation. The human spirit comes into existence when the sperm enters the womb, when the sperm is prepared to receive the soul…"

Ghazali shares many such insights on the spirit most of which can be summarized as:

a) The SPIRIT essentially is not a creation, it is eternal, self-subsisting and ONE.

b) The SPIRIT, independent of the human body, is a single force, it is not many. In other words, there is no such and such person's spirit, ultimately there is only ONE spirit.

c) With the body, the spirit gains certain qualities which stay with the spirit when it leaves the body. Due to these qualities, we may talk about such and such person's spirit, in this sense the spirit becomes seemingly many.

Another noble intimate of the reality who sheds light on the spirit is Abdulqadir al-Jilani.

Gaws al-Azam Abdulqadir al-Jilani says, in his "Qasida-i Ayniyyah":

"I blew into him from my Spirit" is a metaphor! O argumentative one, is not the SPIRIT nothing other than the ONE? The ONE is free from entering into something! For there is no other than HIM! Everything is bound by HIS ONENESS! O the One in the guise of multitude! O the Creator of all things! It is the origin of your Essence that forms all things!"

As can be seen, both from Ghazali's and Jilani's Works, significant explanations regarding the Spirit have been made in the past.

For those who are interested, in his Perfect Man, Jilani gives extensive information on the spirit in the section on "The Angel called Spirit" and "Ruh al-Quds" known as the "Grand Spirit" in Sufism.

Now let us examine the meaning of the Spirit in modern terms.

The being referred to as the "SPIRIT" is by origin a SINGLE force that comprises the essence of everything.

Everything you know, can think of or beyond your comprehension, is made of this SPIRIT.

The best way to understand this is with this analogy:

34

"Matter" is composed of atoms. Regardless of what we call it, what name we give it, it is composed of atoms. When we delve into the depths of the sub-atomic levels of the atoms we encounter "energy" …

This energy is an indivisible, infinite force, for it is made of the power of Allah!

In respect to the Absolute Essence of Allah, 'energy' is a creation (its existence depends on Allah) and in the past it was called the SPIRIT.

The "Spirit" is the manifestation of the "Power" of Allah and it is also known as the "First Intellect", "Universal Consciousness" or "Cosmic Consciousness"!

The consciousness within every individual is derived from this Spirit. However, it manifests according to the capacity and capability of the individual.

When "Spirit" reaches various levels of density it takes different forms and shapes thus creating the illusion of multitude!

Essentially, as Jilani also asserts, the Spirit is an Angel. Everything and anything in the corporeal worlds derive its essence from this Angel! It comprises the origin and essence of all things including all other angels!

Think of an exhibition where there are countless objects made of ice… humans, animals, furniture etc… Although they have different shapes and figures and seem to be different objects, essentially, they are all made of the same thing… water, gas (H_2O). The essence and origin of all of them are atoms!

Similarly, despite the seeming multitude of forms in this grand exhibition called the universe, the essence and origin of everything is a single force; "energy" which, was referred to in the past as the SPIRIT.

6

"THE HUMAN SPIRIT"

With the cosmic effects received by the fetus on the 120th day after conception the activity explained as "the blowing of the spirit by the angel" i.e. wave production commences.

This substance which comprises the core of the brain receives its first cosmic programming, allowing the evaluation of its genetic database to take place, hence the direction of its programming is determined.

This is the instance at which "individual spirit" or "the human spirit" is formed, or created! Before this point the personalized, human spirit does not exist!

It is precisely because of this that abortion after the 120th day is considered to be murder!

For, the core of the brain begins to produce the 'wave body' that is, the 'human spirit' on the 120th day after conception takes place, hence if the fetus is aborted after this, the spirit that has been created will continue its life indefinitely…

The primary characteristics of the person is determined by the genetic code it inherits…

The genetic code is like the seed, and the astrological code is like the factors that allow this seed to grow and develop, like soil, water, sunlight etc.

The brain continuously uploads and backs up all its data to a holographic wave body we call the spirit.

This holographic body is not much different to television waves… Just as television waves are basically carrier waves that carry sound waves and visual waves, the human spirit also carries all the data that is produced by brain activity…

The event called death, when brain function and the magnetic field of the body shuts down, the person continues to live through his holographic wave body…

This is the situation referred to as "resurrection after death"!

However, one will not find anything in that body other than what he thought, felt, feared, loved during his life on earth!

In other words, the identity one forms within his physical biological body on Earth is the one he will continue with after death…

The Rasul of Allah (saw) points to this with his words:

"However, you live and in which ever state you die, that is how you will be resurrected after death and on Doomsday"

Resurrection after death takes place immediately after the experience of the death of the physical body…

In respect of the consciousness life continues without interference, only a transition is made from the biological body into the spirit-wave body…

Because of this I frequently stress the point that after one "tastes i.e. experiences death" they will feel as though they are being buried alive with their spirit body! They will be **fully conscious** at this point!

And until doomsday they will continue to live in the realm of the grave!

The expressions "resurrection after death" in "Amantu" clearly validates that resurrection takes place immediately after death, not on Doomsday!

To better understand the meaning of Allah's name al-Baith which is the force that drives resurrection you can see Imam Ghazali's commentary on the Names of Allah…

As we established, **"the human spirit"**; as of the 120th day, is constantly formed and updated with all the mental products of the brain that take place during the person's entire life, and after this the spirit disconnects from the biological body and continues its life with this accumulated energy and data indefinitely...

As of Doomsday, the spirits that live in the Intermediary Realm which is the radial, wave-based twin of the earth, either become stuck within the radial-twin of the Sun (hell) due to inadequate energy, or escape this magnetic pull and move on to the radial counterparts of the other stars within the galaxy (heaven).

But let us be mindful of the Quranic expression that a single day of the afterlife is equivalent to a thousand earth years... The Rasul of Allah (saw) says the passing over the Bridge of Sirat will take 3000 years alone...

If a single day of the afterlife is 1000 earth years, then you do the math to discern how long 3000 years of the afterlife is!

Hence it is imperative to take a broader perspective on things...

What we associate to the spirit are things that pertain to the brain. This is why the spirit cannot be sick. It is fallacious to think of sickness of the soul. There is only sickness and dysfunctionality of the brain.

Since every brain produces its own spirit with its own waves, when that brain is no longer functional, that spirit cannot move to another brain, this is inconceivable.

Hence reincarnation, the belief that the spirit comes back to the world with a new body is a complete delusion! It is nothing other than the trickery of the jinn...

You may recite the Quran and send prayers to the soul of a deceased person... If that person has received the relevant data during his life on earth, he will be able to receive and evaluate it. Otherwise, the energy carried in the message you send will only give a very temporary relief.

A frequently asked question is, since the realm of the grave lasts billions of years and the person will be conscious and alive in the spirit form, there won't be any suffering, so then what is the torment of the grave?

The person in the grave is as alive and as conscious as he is in this world... He can see both himself and his surroundings. When various bugs, insects, mice, snake etc. under the soil start to eat his face and cheeks, he is going to experience it as real as he would if he were alive on earth. For, throughout his whole life he identified with his body and believed that he is his body, and this belief has automatically been uploaded and saved in his spirit, or consciousness… so he will inevitably experience things with this consciousness and hence feel immense pain and torture!

Take your sleep for example, if you've had a frighting experience during the day and spent your day fearing something, you will most probably see that thing in your dream and continue to feel the same fear even though nothing is happening to your physical body.

There are three stages to the life of the grave:

1. Life inside the grave
2. Life inside the "Realm of the Grave"
3. Life inside the "Intermediary Realm"

You can find detailed information on the 2nd and 3rd stages in *Muhammad's Allah*.

As for the first, life inside the grave, if certain precautions are not taken then it will become an utter nightmare, one from which you cannot wake up! This is known, in religious terms, as "the suffering of the grave".

Just as your day and level of consciousness reflect to your dreams and you can't do anything to change those dreams, the life of the grave is similarly automated, it is the automatic output of your level of consciousness while you are in this world and can no longer be changed.

It is possible to protect yourself from this endless state of pain and suffering by taking certain precautions and making preparations while you are still here, which is the whole point of religion.

In other words, the purpose of religion is not to deify an imaginary god but to duly prepare for an infinite life awaiting after death, to know one's essential reality and to try to understand the reality of Allah![10]

---

[10] More information on this can be found in *The Power of Prayer*.

Spiritual strength is nothing other than the strength of the brain waves, i.e. the frequency your brain outputs, because the waves your brain produces are what forms your spirit.

As for the enlightened ones...

An enlightened saint engages in heavy dhikr and abstinence practices, as a result of this he gains enormous brain capacity and emanates powerful frequencies...

When you find someone like this, they can direct those waves to your brain, whereby a dormant capacity becomes activated in your brain and you will suddenly and easily realize and discern things you weren't able to prior to this experience... Their words will have an impact on you due to the force it carries, and hence this person will stimulate great development in you... and based on this many will say "I went to such and such enlightened person and through him I gained insight and wisdom."

There are two types of brain waves:

1. General waves

2. Directed waves

All brains pre-dominantly output general waves...

Prayer, on the other hand, generates 'directed waves'[11]

For example, a group of people come together and pray for rain, in other words they are all consciously focusing on the same purpose at the same time and collectively producing strong waves that form a magnetic field in that area pulling the clouds together for rain...

---

[11] Detailed information on this can be found in *The Power of Prayer.*

It is the same thing when a group of people come together and consciously and collectively pray together directing their brain waves towards a specific outcome...

Pilgrimage is a much stronger form of this![12]

If many people, even if they are at different places, tune in at the same time with the same intention and concentrate and pray for a specific outcome, it will most probably happen. This is 'spiritual' support!

Sometimes this type of practice may also be directed to other frequencies, such as the jinn, but I do not wish to talk about this here.

THE MEN OF THE UNKNOWN (al-rijal al-ghayb), people of extreme spiritual strength, generally spread various knowledge on earth via these waves...

This is why certain knowledge was acquired and applied at the same time in different locations in the world by people who had no contact with one another... Ibn Arabi metaphorically discusses this in his "al-Futuhat al-Makkiyah" for those who are interested.

The word spirit expresses two significant qualities to us:

1. Spirit is the quintessential energy that comprises the essence of matter, what science calls photons today; it is the universal quantum field!

Hence every iota of existence is composed of the SPIRIT...

There is nothing in the universe that does not derive its existence from the SPIRIT.

Every radial particle or wave exists and moves with the energy it gets from the SPIRIT.

Therefore, the universe has come about with the SPIRIT, it continues to exist with the SPIRIT, and until the Doomsday it will continue to derive its life from the SPIRIT.

In religious terms, the universe was created with the SPIRIT and hence it can never become totally non-existent.

---

[12] More information on this can be found in *The Human Enigma*.

2. The essence or SPIRIT that comprises every quanta is also the source of consciousness within every unit of existence. Hence, everything in the universe is conscious, albeit consciousness itself is indivisible.

Therefore, every activity that transpires in the universe, far from coincidental, is conscious and deliberate, despite how disorderly it may seem at times.

Even the animals, plants, and the cells that we may think are not 'conscious' have individual consciousness and act in a specified order. However, they are not aware of this themselves, and as long as we remain confined to our sensory perception, we cannot become aware of it either.

Here is a verse from the Quran to validate this:

> **"There is nothing that does not exalt** (tasbih) **Him with hamd** (evaluation of the corporeal worlds created with His Names, as He wills)**! But you do not perceive their functions!"**[13]

Indeed, it is impossible for one who limited by his five senses to discern the reality of the quants, its relation to consciousness, and the order in which they operate. It may only be 'known', but not duly understood!

Here is a verse from the Quran regarding the spirit:

> **"And they** (the Jews) **ask you,** (O Muhammad) **about the spirit. Say, "The spirit is from the command** (amr; the manifestation of the Names) **of my Rabb. And you have been given little of this knowledge** (this answer is for the Jews who asked this question).**"**[14]

A renowned scholar of recent centuries, Ismail Haqqi Bursawi, construes this verse in one of his works. Bursawi notes that the word "qalil" comes from the root word "iqlal" which means "to reduce/remove something" hence the verse means, "regarding the spirit, everyone will have knowledge **according to their capacity**" …

---

[13] Quran 17:44
[14] Quran 17:85

43

When the miniscule radial particles we call the photons come together in a specific sequence and amount they form the essence of humans and jinn, and when this composition densifies to a certain degree it forms their different levels and types. However, some partially conscious photons form the type of consciousness we see most commonly in humans.

Among all the countless creations in the universe, humans and jinn have the level of consciousness and hence 'spirit' that can be evaluated by humans.

What differentiates humans from others is the capacity and strength of consciousness and the density of their composition, which makes them bound to the laws of 'matter'.

The following information is from the reputable interpretation of the Quran (Hak Dini Kur'an Dili) by the distinguished scholar Elmalili Hamdi Yazir. Note that it is completely aligned with my explanations:

Regarding the spirit, there are three main definitions;

- The initiator of an action

- The power of life

- The inception of understanding

The spirit, as an initiator of an action, is the power that forms matter. What gives direction and form to matter, is therefore the spirit. For example, electricity, based on this definition, as well as everything that gives form and direction to matter, is spirit.

The spirit, defined as the power of life, is different to this. It is broader in its scope to the spirit defined as the initiator of an action; it is the source of all life throughout existence. It manifests itself even through vegetation and all animal and human life. The spirit carries a greater scope as it manifests itself through humans.

The spirit, in its final definition encompasses traits such as causality, contemplation, knowledge, will power, and the ability to explain, that pertain to humanity. For this reason, it has been called the human spirit, also commonly referred to as consciousness.

What differentiates the human spirit from the animal spirit is its capacity to observe its essential reality. For this reason, the Quran states 'and breathed into Him from my spirit'. We recognize this spirit through our conscience, will power, and desire to observe and know our essence. Had the spirit had not been of a greater potential than what manifests through human awareness, we would not have had the capacity to discern the reality of matter and existence no matter the depth of our knowledge. This spirit, as the source of understanding, is the source of man's corporeality, but it is also man's creations program, his capacity or incapacity to observe the reality of existence and beyond. (Hak Dini, Vol: 4; Page: 3198-3199)

7

THE MAKE-UP OF MAN

The **"HUMAN"** being can be examined from three perspectives:

1. **Human** is the embodiment of consciousness known in Sufism as the "Radial Spirit" …

2. **Spirit body** is "A radial-wave based body in a holographic appearance"[15] In Sufism, it is the life force that drives the biological body called the *animal spirit* which reflects externally as one's aura.

3. **The physical body** is the biological vehicle that houses and carries the brain -the producer of the holographic wave body- i.e. the human spirit…

Now let us explore each of these in further detail:

HUMAN

The being referred to as a 'human' is essentially the embodiment of consciousness…

This consciousness is produced by the brain. The genetic data in the brain together with the cosmic astrological effects, the conditionings it receives, and the thought system that is born from these form the "self-consciousness" i.e. "I'ness" or one's personality.

---

[15] Detailed information on the holographic wave body called the spirit can be found in The Human Enigma on the section on the spirit.

The brain produces all of the above and uploads it to the wave body called the spirit, with which it continues its eternal life.

Consciousness is both the wave body itself and separate from it. If the wave body didn't exist, the brain would still have produced all of the above but the personality will have come to an end with death, when the brain stops functioning, and there would be no afterlife. But the fact that it produces the wave body called the spirit and uploads all its info as a backup to this spirit makes the human consciousness immortal.

The individuality or the wave body continues its life with the Absolute Spirit.

If one can find his self at the level of consciousness, he will know himself at the state of "cosmic consciousness" and reach the speed of thought which is many times faster than the speed of light... it is impossible to explain this state in words.

It does not matter how much the individual consciousness knows or feels himself to be at the level of "cosmic consciousness" his 'individuality' will not be removed with this knowing.

Only once the personality is actually surpassed one may make a leap in consciousness to the level of cosmic consciousness...

The word 'self' or 'ego' refers to the consciousness at the level of the individuality.

Its original form is the "Purified Self (nafs al-safiyah).

The cosmic consciousness at the level of the Purified Self after becoming prone to conditioning and developing values, judgments and emotions that arise from these, becomes veiled and falls from his essential reality to the level of the Inciting Self (nafs al-ammarah) ...

The "Self" (nafs) is the I'ness, the consciousness of one's 'personhood'; it is the illusory identity. The extent to which one is cleansed of this illusion, the self may return to its origin and unite with Allah...

SPIRIT

Spirit is the wave body with which the immortal being called 'human' continues his eternal life... Its holographic in appearance and is a concise backup of the brain waves produced during one's life on earth.

When the bioelectrical energy that runs in the nervous system is cut off, the magnetic pull of the body dissipates, allowing the spirit to detach itself and commence a life free of the biological body - the event called death.

The wave body both receives its energy from the brain and supplies energy to the brain... Like the motor of a car that receives its energy from the car battery while at the same time charging it.

When the spirit leaves the body and doesn't return, the brain becomes deprived of this energy and stops functioning, i.e. the event we call death takes place...

The memory unit of the brain is the data in the wave body... The brain accesses this memory unit in the spirit when it needs to... When the brain begins to dysfunction it can't access the data in the wave body and hence "forgetfulness" starts to take place...

The attraction and repulsion that occurs between spirits is because of the elementary make-up of the cosmic astrological effects received, and the four different frequencies that are produced based on these elements, namely, earth – fire – water – air.

The appearance of the wave body is exactly like a hologram, and the spirit is upon its last image, just before death takes place...

If for example, a man whose had his arm amputated at the age of thirty dies at the age of fifty, he will find his hologram body with an arm, just as it was before it was amputated. For no information uploaded to the spirit ever disappears.

Because all of the qualities uploaded to the spirit are produced by the brain, the more we are able to expand our brains capacity and the more energy we produce, is the stronger our spirit will be...

This is why it has been said, "The world is the sowing field of the hereafter, whatever you sow here that is what you will reap there"

"Worship" is specifically for this purpose, to enhance, expand and develop the brain. The anti-magnetic force produced and uploaded to the spirit by the brain was, in religious terms, called "NUR (light)". Hence the strength and amount of the anti-magnetic force that is uploaded to the spirit is the primary determinant of whether or not one can escape the pull of the Sun on doomsday.

If the person neglected this practice of uploading energy to his spirit he will not be able to save himself from the strong magnetic pull of the Sun and will become stuck within it forever.

The structure that carries the personal consciousness is the wave body, it is like television waves that carry image and sound waves… It is a mobile structure and is free from the concepts of time and space, it can co-exist at multiple places at the same time.

Its greatest quality is its ability to delve into the core of whatever situation it encounters to search for and seek its reality. Since our personal consciousness is inside this structure we call the spirit, all of the qualities of one's consciousness is perceived from this structure…

It is the bioelectrical energy produced by the brain, the energy which holds all the cells together and preserves the integral makeup of the body.

THE BODY

What we all know and perceive as a 'human'…

It has numerous functions…

First, it forms the human consciousness…

Secondly, it supplies the bioelectrical energy through the digestion process. The energy it attains from the process of breaking down and digesting food, is transferred to the brain, and the brain transforms this into bioelectrical energy…

Thirdly, the magnetic energy that holds all the cells together and prevents the body from falling apart is produced by the physical brain…

When the person who is essentially clothed in a body of waves is disconnected and separated from the spirit, the cells that form the body begin to lose their attraction to one another and hence they disintegrate and begin to deteriorate, whereby each cell transforms into a compound closest to its programming…

All forms of pain that arise in the body reflect a dysfunction of the organs due to either an internal or an external factor… this is felt through the pain centers in the brain…

If these centers stop functioning or are temporarily rendered inactive through hypnosis or other means, the person won't feel any pain in his body…

The reason why a 'human' feels pain is because the brain is too busy processing the data causing the 'pain' and is hence unable to do its actual job, which is to manifest the qualities and the wants of the "human."

Whereas when this mission is not accomplished, due to bodily pain and suffering, the person feels the pain of not being able to manifest his desires at the material level. But because we don't know this, we think the pain is stemming from the body.

What people call undeveloped or primitive soul, is the interface of the brain not working properly and hence not being able to manifest the qualities of man at the material level…

That is, all ailments associated to the malfunctioning of the intellect or the soul are born from the inadequacy of the brain or a pathologic change that causes brain malfunction…

The ability of a human to produce and output activity aligned with his capabilities and skills depends on his brain development, which depends on various internal and external conditions.

When what we call "morals" are damaged leading to behavior that goes against the best interest of a person or a society, again it is the brain at play. The reason for the damaging behavior in this case is because the brain, which causes these attributes to move from 'human' to 'body' loses some of its neural connections in the relative areas and hence the brain become incohesive.

In this case, the radial body of man, the animal spirit, can intervene and remove the blockages in the brain or supply the necessary electromagnetic force to enable the required neural connections.

The reason why man will be held accountable for his immoral behavior is because immorality does not exist in his essential being, it comes from an insufficient usage of the brain, because of this it is his responsibility to fix it.

Everyone is created upon a perfect form. Here is a verse to prove this:

"We have certainly created man in the best of forms (with the qualities of the Names)."[16]

Indeed, humans have been created upon the best of forms, then restricted via their wave-body, then their biological body and hence their brain, and left to manifest the perfection embedded within in this material platform… The extent to which he accomplishes this he will be rewarded and the extent to which he fails he will deserve its consequence… The following verse validates the material restriction after being created upon a perfect form:

"Then We reduced him to the lowest of the low (to his world of conditionings)."[17]

As can be seen, even though every one is created upon a perfect form if he doesn't actualize this capacity by developing his brain, he won't be able to manifest and display his qualities and hence will be held accountable by his creator.

As I said above **moral corruption** is also the result of certain pathological disorders in the brain. Here is what the distinguished Professor Doctor Sadi Irmak says about the brain:

"Regarding the frontal cortex of the brain this is what we know: There are 15 billion neurons in the shell of the forebrain and there are fibers that connect these neurons together, and there are also electrical connections… Recent evidence shows that a human being (with an approximate life span of 90 years) uses only a minimal part of these possible connections. These neural connections are what allows and enables contemplation and philosophical understanding…

---

[16] Quran 95:04
[17] Quran 95:05

But we now know that even those with the most developed of brains, such as Einstein, died having only used a very small part of these connective fibers...

Here are some assumptions:

With time humans are going to get used to or be forced to make new neural connections and hence develop new capabilities...

In fact, if one day all the connections between the 15 billion cells are made active, humans will come very close to divinity, they will be the shadow or the vicegerent of Allah... But for now, we seem to be very far from this point... Of course, the ordinary person uses maybe five or ten of these neural connections... Shakespeare's vocabulary was six thousand words, while a villager knows only 60 words... The number of words one uses also reflects his usage of these neural connections... One who has a richer vocabulary has richer neural connectivity...

Does every single word reflect a neural connection?

Yes... Every single word reflects a neural connection, as different neural groups are connected for every word....

Does the evolution of man depend on the usage of these fibers?

Yes, in fact it does, anatomically these fibers are present in everyone, but its usage depends on the person's capacity... Not encountering situations that force one to activate and use these connections may also be a reason... the more they are not used the more one's insight becomes blinded...

So, then someone with a rich imagination is actually someone who uses a lot of neural connections?

Yes, this is one of the outcomes of knowledge! Hence it is extremely important to raise children with exercises that activate and stimulate mental growth..."

Since this is not intended to be a medical book, I shall not go into any more detail about the properties of the brain... but I'm sure the words of Turkey's most distinguished professor would have had some impact on validating my point ...

What I call human, the religious texts call "self" (nafs) and man. Some religious books also use terms like "the real spirit" or "the observing spirit".

This is how we construe words, if you read the below excerpt carefully you will see there is no contradiction between my view and those of renowned scholars such as Ibn Abbas.

The below is from the 9th volume of Elmalili's "Hak Dini Kuran Dili":

"NAFS, means the being, the self of everything. It also means the soul and the heart. In the context of religion, it refers to the inception point of all suffering. Hereunder it references the first definition." (Vol:1/Page:223)

Every soul (NAFS) will experience death. NAFS refers to the soul and being, and from this certain have understood this to confirm the immortality of the soul. For 'experience' implicates a continuation of life. The pleasure of experience also insinuates being alive.

In which case the meaning becomes: "Every nafs will experience the death of the body."

This means that the soul and the body are separate and the death of the body does not mean the death of the soul. Therefore, the concept known as death belongs to the body, while the soul is eternal." (Vol 2: page 1244)

According to Hadrath Ibn-i Abbas, the mental prowess to differentiate between right and wrong is attributed to the nafs' power of thought. This is directly associated with the soul, not the body and it is eternal.

"Hadrath Ibni Abbas has said: Humanity is made up of the ego and the soul; their difference is like the sun and the light that it emits. The ego serves the processes of thought and judgement. With death, both are separated from the body, while at sleep only the personality is separated." (Vol 5/Page 4127)

The angel of death (the power of death) cuts off the body's life energy. It separates the consciousness from the body and sustains its existence as the soul. (Vol 5/Page: 4129)

8

THE REALITY OF DEATH

Sadly, for many, the reality of **death** is unknown; it is thought of as an **end**. Far from it! **Death** is a transition from the material dimension to the immaterial dimension. It is a transformation.

With **death**, the person leaves his material body and continues to live with his **holographic radial-wave body**, i.e. **spirit** in the grave or beyond it. In short, death is the end of life with the material body to commence a life with the spirit body. The Quran brings clarity to the process known as death with the following verse:

> **"Every individual consciousness will taste death** (life without a biological body will continue eternally) **..."** (Quran 3:185)

Death is abandoning the biological material body to live **with the spirit body** at the level of waves.

When the brain ceases to function, the electromagnetic energy, which keeps the spirit connected to the body, stops being supplied, causing the spirit to detach and continue its life independent of the body. This is the event we refer to as **death**.

Since every activity that occurs in the brain throughout one's lifetime is uploaded to the holographic wave body (as television waves are through audio and visual waves) the person will continue his life as the spirit without feeling any difference. He will live as the spirit and won't feel any difference in terms of the continuity of his life, albeit for one exception. He will not be able to use his physical body despite being completely alive and conscious! It will be as though he is in a coma or in a vegetative state, whereby he can see, hear and perceive everything that is happening around him, yet he is unable to show any response!

In his acclaimed *Marifatname*, Ibrahim Hakki Erzurumi narrates the following about death, in the words of Muhammad (saw):

"The deceased will know who washes and shrouds his body, who partakes in his funeral prayer, who puts him down in his grave, and who offers condolences."

The warning **'Do not beat your chest and cry out loud near your dead, as by doing this you will be torturing them'** is again alluding to the fact that the deceased are able to hear and become grieved by all the mourning.

Perhaps the Bukhari collection of hadith comprises the most explicate narrations in clarifying the reality of death and life after death. There are many hadith affirming that the deceased, though unable to use his physical body, will be fully aware and conscious in the grave as the **spirit** and will be able to perceive all that transpires around him. Here is an example:

Narrated by Talha (r.a.):

The day of the battle of *Badr*, Rasulullah (saw) ordered us to gather the corpse of twenty of *Quraysh*'s notable men and throw their bodies down a dirty well. As such, the dirty well had gathered more dirt.

It was Rasulullah's (saw) custom to spend three nights on the field of battle once he was victorious over the enemy. So, on the third day after the battle of *Badr*, Rasulullah (saw) asked for his camel. We tied his bag to the camel and Rasulullah (saw) began to walk as we followed him. The men talked amongst each other trying to guess where Rasulullah (saw) was going. Finally, he stopped by the well in which we had thrown the corpses and called out to them with their fathers' names.

"O such and such, o Aba Jahl ibn Hisam, o Utba ibn Rabia... If you had believed in and obeyed Allah and His Rasul, would you have been happy now? O slayed ones! We truly found the victory promised by our *Rabb*. Did you also find the victory promised by your *Rabb* to be the truth?"

Upon this, Omar (r.a.) asked Rasulullah (saw) "O Rasulullah, why do you talk to the corpses who are dead?"

Rasulullah (saw) answered:

"By the One in whose hands the soul of Muhammad is, you do not hear my words better than they do!"

As can be seen from this hadith, Rasulullah (saw) is trying to correct a big misunderstanding regarding death. No other hadith can correct the misconception that **people are dead when placed into their graves and will only be resurrected back to life on Doomsday.** Indeed, **people will be as aware and conscious as they are now when they are buried and will be able to hear everything that is told to them, just as they would if they were outside.**

The third Khalifa Osman bin Affan (r.a.) stood near a grave he would cry until his beard got soaked. Someone once said to him "You do not weep when you hear about heaven and hell but you cry in fear of the grave". He replied: "I heard Rasulullah (saw) say:

'**The grave is the first station of the afterlife, if one is able to pass this station the rest of his journey will be easier, but if one cannot pass this station, the rest of his journey will be much difficult.'**"

Then he added, "Rasulullah (saw) said,

'**I have never encountered a scene more frightening than that of the grave.'**"

Standing before the grave of one of Islam's most distinguished martyrs, Sa'd bin Muaz, who Rasulullah (saw) buried with his own hands, Rasullulah (saw) said:

"This eminent soul for whom the throne (*arsh*) trembled and the gates of the heavens opened and thousands of angels descended... Even he frets so much in his grave that his bones were almost going to crumble. If anyone were to escape from the torments of the grave and the anguish after death, this would have been possible for Sa'd first! Though, due to the elevated rank he had acquired here, he was swiftly released!"

Let us now consider, if the person isn't aware and conscious in his grave, could such torments be possible?

It was asked to Rasulullah (saw): "O Rasulullah, which of the believers are more intelligent and more conscious?" He answered:

"Those who remember the reality of death most often and who prepare for the after death most prudently. Indeed, they are the most intelligent and conscious ones."

In yet another narration, he says: **"The most conscious and prudent one is he who subjects his soul to the divine laws and engages in deeds that will benefit him in the hereafter. The impotent one is he who follows his desires then hopes for salvation from Allah!"**

Ibn Masud, one of the followers of Rasulullah (saw) says:"I had heard Rasulullah (saw) say **'the sinners will assuredly be tormented in their graves, in fact even the animals will hear their anguish!'"**

Abu Said al Hudri narrates:

I heard Rasulullah say:

"The denier will be tormented by ninety-nine dragons that will sting and bite him until the Day of Judgment. If only one of these dragons were to blow on earth, no green plant would ever live again."

Ibn Omar (r.a.) narrates:

Rasulullah (saw) said:

"When a person dies, his place, whether it be heaven or hell, will be shown to him every morning and every evening. He will be told, 'this is your place, until the Day of Judgment, when you will be resurrected, you will be here.'"

Another interesting note is the statement *"wal bat'thu ba'dal **mawt**"* in *Amantu*, which literally means "… and in resurrection after **death**", it does not say "resurrection after **Doomsday**"! Evidently, *ba'th*, i.e. **resurrection**, is an event that occurs after tasting death, not after Doomsday!

We live in this world with our physical bodies and the spirit body that we simultaneously produce.

When one tastes of death, the material body will dissolve and the spirit will resurrect and continue to live in the grave until Doomsday.

When Doomsday occurs, that is, the instance that the earth is engulfed in the radioactive heat of the sun…

And finally, our bodies will also be resurrected appropriate to the environment to which they will go.

Will we work with the same mind and perception mechanisms we have here in our graves?

In regards to this, Abdullah bin Omar (r.a.) narrates the following:

When Rasulullah (saw) was talking about *Munkir* and *Nakir*, the two angels who will call the person to account in his grave, Hadhrat Omar (r.a.) asked: **"Are we going to be conscious in our graves, O Rasulullah?"**

"Indeed, exactly as you are today," Rasulullah (saw) answered.

So, what happens when a person, who is fully aware and conscious, yet whose body has become dysfunctional, is placed the grave?

Let us see how Anas (r.a.) has to say about this:

Rasulullah (saw) said:

"When the person is placed in his grave, he will hear the footsteps of those who buried him moving further and further away. Then the two angels will come and ask him: 'What do you say about the man Muhammad?'

If the person is a believer he will say 'I bear witness that Muhammad is Allah's servant and Rasul.' Then they will ask 'Look at your place in hell, Allah has transformed it into paradise for you.' From that point on, he will see both his place in hell and the place he will go to in heaven.

If he is a denier or a hypocrite disguised as a Muslim, he will say 'I do not have a definite opinion, I only know of what others used to say.' They will say to him 'You have failed to recognize and know him!' and then they will hit him with a hammer with such intensity that the whole of creation except man and the jinni will hear his anguish!"

Let us now end this topic with a final hadith:

"The deceased one will be tormented by the lamenting of his relatives and friends."

There are many more warning of Rasulullah (saw) pertaining to this topic. Those who are interested may consult the appropriate hadith books.

The point is, **the person does not die, he merely experiences death!**

To experience death is to lose control over one's material body and to continue living with a sort of holographic wave body, termed **spirit**.

Therefore, everyone who is buried is fully conscious and aware! And they will exist in this state until Doomsday, after which they will be equipped with new bodies according to the environment and conditions of that time and place.

Such is the life awaiting us on the other side!

9

THE MAKE-UP OF THE JINN AND THEIR COMMON ATTRIBUTES

The 'jinn' who can sometimes appear as matter even though they are commonly imperceivable by the human eye, are of two types:

1. Jinn... Forms of consciousness that are outside the spectrum of human perception.

2. The Animal Spirit - Hologram body

Jinn

The jinn are conscious beings, commonly known as ghosts, spirits, entities, etc., who commonly delude people into thinking they are aliens or the spirits of people who have passed away.

They derive their self-consciousness or "I-ness" from the SPIRIT as I have explained in previous chapters.

In terms of their level of consciousness they are inferior to humans...

In order for a jinn to *know* itself it needs a wave body, a hologram, which when given, marks their birth...

In the absolute sense, their death takes place during Doomsday, as is the case with humans...

In the simple and general sense, their death, similar to humans, happens when they leave their hologram body at the end of their determined life span…

Even though their span of life is similar to humans, due to their make-up and attributes, it can last up to 700-1000 years, according to our concept of time. According to theirs, this feels like 60-70 years…

Due to their make-up, they have many advanced qualities, despite this, their level of consciousness is much lower than humans… A human with a high level of consciousness is much superior in level than a jinn with an advanced level of consciousness.

Their characteristic make-up is simpler and more primitive than humans. They display what we call unfavorable or negative behavior very frequently. They usually engage in adverse and destructive activity. However, among them there are also religious and devout jinn, and sometimes, though rarely, saints.

Their biggest entertainment is causing mischief among the weaker humans to possess and manipulate them for their own cause.

All attributes commonly associated with "Satan" actually belong to the jinn. As "satanism" is an attribute of the jinn; there is no "Satan" besides the jinn.

We will explore the qualities and attributes of the jinn in more detail in the following chapters. For now, let us examine their hologram body.

Because the jinn are not bound by matter as we know it, they have access to information of the past… As for the future, again due to their make up, they have some insight as to what may transpire but they don't know for sure, they definitely don't know in detail, and as a matter of fact, most times they are inaccurate.

The Animal Spirit – Hologram Body

The make up this hologram body is composed of waves that has not yet been scientifically discovered. Though I believe it won't be too difficult to detect by the qualified if they work on it…

These waves the same qualities as the human wave body explained in previous sections...

The functions of their body are uploaded to the hologram body, they can appear as matter when they please, and they are not bound by time and space...

They have the mobility and speed to be anywhere in the world they like.

But how does their life span last 1000 years?

As aforementioned, the lifespan of the jinn is approximately 10-13 times the average human life span, i.e. 700-1000 years... Some are known to live up to 1400 years...

They owe the longevity of their life span to their make-up and 'velocity', which is much higher than that of humans...

Let me try to explain this in the light of science...

In physics there is a phenomenon whereas velocity increases time slows down... When velocity reaches a particular threshold, time stops altogether.

Distinguished physicist Paul Langevin describes this as the famous twin paradox:

"This remark gives a way, for any of us, who is willing to devote two years of his life, of knowing how the Earth will be in two hundred years time, to explore the future of the Earth, by hopping forward in the history of the latter, of two centuries, corresponding in his own life to only two years; but without any hope of return, without the possibility to come and inform us of the result of his journey, because any similar attempt can only throw him further and further into the future.

It is sufficient for this that our traveler agrees to shut himself up in a projectile, sent away from the Earth, with a speed sufficiently close to that of light, although less, which is physically possible, arranging that an encounter occurs with, for example, a star, after one year in the life of the traveler, that sends the spaceship back towards the Earth with the same speed. Returning to Earth, having aged by two years, he will climb out of his vehicle and find our globe aged by at least two hundred years, if his speed had stayed within an interval of less than twenty-thousandth of the speed of light. Established experimental facts of physics allow us to state that the situation will really be as the one just described".[18]

This is due to the acceleration of time…

Indeed, because the jinn are not bound by matter, they exist at an extremely accelerated velocity.

Due to this velocity, they experience what seems 70 years to us in a span of 700 years… Hence, based on our concept of time and velocity we can conclude that the life span of the jinn is ten times the life span of humans, though in their concept of time and space it is like 70 years.

While the jinn live up to what seems like a thousand years to us, the subatomic particles 'pion' (or a pi meson) have a mean lifetime of 26,033 nanoseconds! The u mesons can travel up to a few km, sometimes more than ten km, before they decay or 'die'!

Now the jinn possess several significant attributes, which can also be seen on humans who have inadvertently become possessed by the jinn.

1. The jinn lack logical integrity.

2. The jinn have delusions of grandeur, or 'superiority complex'.

3. The jinn have a very weak self-control mechanism.

4. The jinn frequently repeat themselves.

Regardless of what it's called or where on earth it is encountered, the speech given by the jinn always display these properties.

1. The jinn lack logical integrity.

If you pay attention to the sermons given by the jinn or by "aliens" you can clearly see that there is no logic or coherence in their claims; it is full of contradiction. They jump from one topic to another and to cover their

---

[18] Langevin, 1911, p. 50.

inconsistency they make excuses like "We present these discrepancies to test you and encourage you to contemplate".

The truth is they are full of discrepancies. This is because even though they are astute and quick-witted, they are **intellectually limited**. They can quickly present a solution to the current problem on hand but because of their limited intellect their solution will almost always conflict with either a previous claim or one they will make in the future.

2. The jinn have delusions of grandeur or 'superiority complex'.

Their delusion of grandeur is not only in the egoistical sense but also in terms of physical dimensions.

While they try to present themselves as the governors of earth, they cause confusion among the people using dimensional grandeur. To prove their superiority, they place hierarchy between themselves and humans, going as far as claiming they are from outer space.

The majority of those who believe that the jinn are "aliens" lack fundamental knowledge of Islam and Sufism. They have no insight into what the Quran or the Rasul of Allah (saw) says regarding these topics. Hence, when they encounter these seemingly 'extra-ordinary' stories or experiences they are easily fooled by them.

Moreover, the jinn cause illusory visions and hallucinations making their stories even more compelling to believe.

Another important tactic the jinn use is approaching every society with their specific cultural values and beliefs, thereby making it easier for those populations to believe and accept them.

While their contact with the irreligious is completely different, they approach the devout with religious values or by using the name of an important saint, hence easily deceiving those with pure intentions.

3. The jinn have a very weak self-control mechanism.

Due to their lack of self-control, they easily lose their balance or go too far; they rarely know when and where to stop.

They may start their speech from a seemingly sophisticated high-level but before you know it, they inadvertently reveal their primitiveness.

Sometimes they go as far as claiming they are the creators of the Creator, at other times they claim they have personified and embodies Allah and sent Him down to earth, and sometimes they claim to be the devout servants of Allah whilst doing everything they can to divert the believers away from religion and the teachings of the Rasul of Allah (saw).

4. The jinn frequently repeat themselves.

While they constantly preach to the people to impose their superiority the jinn intermittently repeat themselves or repeat their sentences.

Most of their sermons consist of the same sentences with perhaps one or two different words.

My understanding of why this may be is:

1. Repeating certain words, like dhikr, enables them to manipulate the neural pathways of the psychics with whom they connect in order to strengthen their bondage.

2. To save time when they have an intellectual block up.

Let us now see what the Quran says about the jinn, the incidents that occurred between the jinn and the Rasul (saw) and the prominent viewpoints on the jinn discussed in various religious sources.

10

THE QURAN ON "THE JINN"

Thus far we explored this topic in light of science… Now let us examine what the Quran and the Rasul of Allah (saw) say about the jinn.

The verses I'm about to share are from "Decoding the Quran - A Unique Sufi Interpretation":

> **And He created the jann**[19] (the invisible beings; the jinn) **from a smokeless flame of fire** (radiation, radiant energy, electromagnetic wave body).[20]

Just as we say 'man is made of earth' in respect of his body, similarly the jinn are made of smokeless fire i.e., radiation.

***

> **"And the jann (a type of jinn) We created before from 'samum' fire (an infusing microwave radiation that is harmful to the astral body)."**[21]

Again, it is describing the body and make-up of the jinn, only this time providing more detail about its nature: a toxic type of fire that infuses or penetrates through matter, i.e., radiation.

---

[19] Sometimes used as the plural form of the word 'jinn'
[20] Quran 55:15
[21] Quran 15:27

Interestingly, Mehmet Hamdi Yazır says:

Therefore, it may conclude that before the creation of man, as was the case before the creation of the Sun and the Earth, there were certain life forces present in the universe, in the form of waves, like pure fire or electricity, able to penetrate through all forms. These forces that are invisible to the human eye are named 'jann'.[22]

***

The Day when He will gather them together (and say), "O community of jinn, you have truly possessed (misled from reality) the vast majority of mankind."[23]

This verse brings an explanation to many unexplained modern-day phenomenon. It reveals the greatest attribute of the jinn; their tendency to manipulate and control humans and bring them under their service.

As previously mentioned, the jinn have a seeming advantage over humans due to their make-up. Their understanding of putting their qualities into effective use is actually an exploitation of their qualities to reign over humans.

Their success and social status among each other actually depend on how many humans they can deceive and bring under their control…

I will provide more detail about their methods of deception in the following chapters.

***

I have created the jinn and men only so that they may serve Me (by means of manifesting the qualities of My Names).[24]

This verse makes it clear that the jinn, like humans, have also been created for the purpose of fulfilling their servitude to their creator.

---

[22] Volume 6, Page 4670
[23] Quran 6:128
[24] Quran 51:56

***

O communities of jinn and man, if you are able to pass beyond the regions of the heavens and the earth, then pass (live without a body)! But you cannot pass unless you possess the power (the manifestation of Allah's attribute of Power [Qadir] on you).[25]

There will be sent upon (both of) you a flame of fire and smoke (ambiguity and confusion in your consciousness), and you will not be successful![26]

And when (during death) the heaven (the identity; ego) is split asunder and (the reality) becomes (undeniably clear and the ego-self disappears) burnt oil colored, like a rose (the reality is observed)![27]

These verses validate the fact that the jinn will also be called to account for their deeds and they too will be subject to the painful consequences of not complying with the commands of their Creator.

***

The word of your Rabb: "I will surely fill Hell completely with the jinn and men" is fulfilled.[28]

This verse tells us that just like humans, the jinn who don't comply with the commands of their Creator will be subject to the suffering of hell upon resurrection after death.

***

And we have appointed for them companions (those with satanic ideas from among the jinn and man) who made attractive to them their actions and desires. And the sentence

---

[25] Quran 55:33
[26] Quran 55:35
[27] Quran 55:37
[28] Quran 11:119

concerning the jinn and man that had passed before them has now come into effect upon them. Indeed, they were all losers.[29]

This verse validates that the jinn are also required to follow the teachings of the Nabis and the Rasuls, and that they too will either be rewarded or punished for their deeds. In fact, this verse implicitly tells us that Nabis and Rasuls were sent to the jinn in the past centuries, perhaps from among humans, whom they were advised to follow.

***

And they have assumed between Him (Allah) and the jinn (conscious beings outside the human capacity of perception) a connection (i.e. associated divinity to them), but the jinn know well that, indeed, they (who made such assumptions) shall surely be summoned (will realize such a connection does not actually exist)![30]

According to this verse, just as a group of people emerged from among the humans claiming that Jesus (pbuh) is the son of Allah, a group of jinn also claimed to have similar ties to Allah.

We can also deduce from this verse that while these jinn were making such claims, there were other jinn among them who knew these allegations were nonsense and that those spreading these lies will be called to account for it. In other words, just as there are jinn who have gone astray from the reality, there are also truly devout believers among the jinn whose lives are aligned with the reality.

***

"From among the jinni (invisible forces) **and man!"**[31]

Based on this verse, just as we seek protection from the evil of humans, we are encouraged to seek refuge and protection from the evil of the jinn, for only then can we truly be shielded from their harm.

***

---

[29] Quran 41:25
[30] Quran 37:158
[31] Quran 114:6

"O communities of jinn and mankind, did there not come to you Rasuls from among you, relating to you My messages pointing to the reality and warning you of the coming of this Day?" They will say, "We bear witness against ourselves"; and the worldly life (they had conjured based on corporeality) had deluded them, and they will bear witness against themselves that they were deniers of the knowledge of the reality.[32]

This verse depicts the state of both humans and jinn on the day of judgment… It also underlines the reality that Nabis and Rasuls were also sent to the jinn and that they too have duties towards their Creator, that they are also responsible for complying with the recommendations of Allah and His Rasul (saw) yet the majority of them do not heed these divine recommendations.

Again, we can clearly see with this verse that when the jinn are faced with the reality they will understand and admit to causing their own demise with their very own hands. Like humans, though the jinn are invited to embrace the reality, the vast majority of them are "coverers of the truth".

***

And We directed to you a group of the jinn (beings outside the human visible spectrum), so they may listen to the Quran… When they were ready for it, they said, "Be silent!" And when it was concluded, they went back to their people as warners.

They said, "O our people, indeed we have heard a knowledge revealed after Moses confirming what was before it, which guides to the Truth and to a straight path (*tariq al-mustaqim*; knowledge that leads to the realization of one's servitude to Allah, with or without their consent).

"O our people, respond to the DAI'ALLAH (the jinn perceived him as the Dai'Allah not the Rasulullah; misused words such as 'messenger' denoting a courier of information derive from this word) and believe in him; Allah will forgive for you some of your sins and protect you from a great suffering…"[33]

---

[32] Quran 6:130
[33] Quran 46:29-31

Note:

The jinn recognized the Rasuls as 'DAI'ALLAH,' which literally means the 'inviters of/to Allah.' The commonly used phrase 'Messenger of Allah,' which denotes a postman position to the Rasuls, also arises from this word.

Here we see for the first time that a group of the jinn listen to the Quran and then go back to their people and call them to faith...

***

1. Say: "It has been revealed to me that a group of the jinn listened (to the Quran) and said, 'Indeed, we have heard an amazing Quran.'"

2. "It guides to the right course (maturity/perfection), so we have believed in it. And we will never associate partners to our Rabb!"

3. "Indeed, exalted is the nobleness of our Rabb; He has not taken a wife or a son!"

4. "Our inadequate understanding has been making us claim foolish things about Allah!"

5. "We had thought that mankind and the jinn would never speak a lie about Allah."

6. "And yet there were men and women from mankind who sought refuge in men and women from the jinn, thereby increasing (provoking each other) in excessive (carnal) behavior."

7. "And they had thought, as you thought, that Allah would never resurrect (*ba'th*) anyone." (This verse indicates that jinn, like humans, have no proficiency pertaining to life after death/resurrection.)

8. "And we touched the heaven but found it filled with powerful guards (forces) and burning flames (rays that impeded our judgment)."

9. "And we used to take up positions therein to listen, but whoever listens now will find a burning flame lying in wait for him."

10. And we do not know whether evil is intended for those on earth (body) or whether their Rabb intends for them a right course (the maturity to observe the reality). (This verse is a clear proof that the jinn have no knowledge of how people will live; how their essential composition of Names will manifest in their lives and what their purpose of manifesting in the sight of Allah is.)

11. "And among us are the righteous, and among us are those who are below (the righteous state); we are of various ways (different breeds/species/races; a cosmopolitan community of different make-up and understanding)."

12. "And we have become certain that we can never invalidate Allah's command upon earth, nor can we escape Him by flight."

13. "When we heard the guidance (Quran), we believed it was the reality. And whoever believes in his Rabb as his own reality, will not fear any deprivation (of his rights) or derogation."

14. "And among us are those in submission, and among us are wrongdoers who rebel against the commands. And those who submit are the aspirants of the fullness of the reality."

15. "But as for the wrongdoers who disobey the commands, they will be firewood for Hell!"[34]

Finally, these verses give us insight into the general behavior of the jinn… This chapter in the Quran, which is called "Chapter al-Jinn" contains very interesting information about the jinn, which if understood and evaluated properly, can give us significant comprehension regarding these beings…

The jinn that is narrating this says, **"When we heard the guidance (Quran), we believed it was the reality"** hence showing us that some of them have faith in the Quran.

---

[34] Quran 72:15

The second point to take note of is **men and women from mankind seeking refuge in men and women from the jinn, thereby increasing (provoking each other) in excessive (carnal) behavior!**

I will cover more on this topic in the following chapters.

Thirdly, we are given important information regarding the place of the jinn in the universe, their actions, their methods of extracting information and the things that burn and harm them... Again, more on this in the following chapters...

The fourth point to consider is their confession regarding their incapacity to know how people will live; how their essential composition of Names will manifest in their lives and what their purpose of manifesting in the sight of Allah is, and hence any information they provide is far from the truth.

And finally, the jinn, like humans, are of different opinions and beliefs; while some deny the reality, some have submitted to and are aspiring to achieve the fullness of the reality.

All of this is let known to us though their own words...

11

HADITH ON "THE JINN"

After sharing the relevant verses from the Quran regarding the **jinn,** let us now examine the two **hadiths** narrated by the Rasul of Allah (saw):

"At that time the **jinn** were unable to receive any information from the heavens. Whenever they attempted, flames of fire were sent onto them. Therefore, a distinguished one among them said:

"Something must have happened recently, clearly a barrier has been put between us and the heavens! Let us navigate the earth to try and understand what has happened."

So, the **jinn** started to search all over the world for the source of the barrier. Those who went towards Tuhama came across the Rasul (saw) at a place called Nakhla, it was on the way to Suq 'Ukaz and the Rasul (saw) was offering the Fajr prayer with his companions. When they heard the Quran, they listened to it and said, "By Allah, this is the thing which has put a barrier between us and the news of heaven." They went back to their people and said, "O our people; verily we have heard a wonderful recital which shows the true path; we believed in it and would not ascribe partners to our Rabb."

It was after this that Allah revealed the chapter al-Jinn to his Rasul (saw).

The second **hadith** narrated by Ibn-i Masood (ra) is:

The Rasul of Allah (saw) said, "I have been ordered to read the Quran to the **jinn,** so who will come with me?"

Everybody was silent. He asked for the second time. There was silence again. He asked for the third time and this time I replied:

-Me, **Abdullah!** O, Rasul of Allah I will come with you.

So, we stood up and walked together.

When we came to the place called Hajoon near Doob Shib, he drew a line in front of me and said:

-Do not go beyond this!

Then, he went towards Hajoon.

They immediately flew over him like partridges. They resembled the 'Zud' group. They were playing their tambourines similar to the way the women played theirs.

In the end, they surrounded him and he was lost from my sight. I stood up immediately from where I was sitting. At that moment, he made a gesture with his hand telling me to 'sit down'. Then, he started to recite the Quran. His voice was becoming louder and louder as he continued reciting. They were all struck to the ground in a way that I was able to hear their voices, though I could not see them.

Later, when the Rasul of Allah came near me, he asked: "You wanted to come with me, didn't you?
I answered, "Yes, O Rasul of Allah!" He said, "It wasn't necessary for you. They are the **jinn!** They came here to listen to the Quran, after which they went back to their community to warn them."

Now based on these hadith we can conclude the following:

1. Normally, the **jinn** were able to ascend to the higher levels (I will explain what I mean by this later) of the heavens and retrieve information regarding events that are to transpire in the future.

2. After the revelation of the Quran or after the duty of **Risalah** was given to Muhammad (saw) the **jinn** were prevented from receiving information from the higher levels of the heavens.

3. From this we may deduce that they could not perceive the entire world at the same time; for this they would need more time.

4. The **jinn** are prevented from obtaining information from the higher levels of the heavens by objects known as **Shihab** (or meteors – objects that fall and burn when they come into contact with the atmosphere).

5. They can make themselves denser and hence assume a material form.

6. Some among them can be given the duty of warning their community.

7. They can make sound that is perceivable by the human ear.

12

THE OPINIONS OF SOME ISLAMIC SCHOLARS

Let us now see what one of the notable scholars of Islam, Imam Abu Hasan al-Ashari, says about the jinn:

"Life that manifests in a large body can also manifest in a single particle. In regards to the reality, life is not an inherent quality of material objects, it is the command of the Rabb. For this reason, large objects may become manifest in a single particle.

The eye can see an object that other people cannot see in spite of the fact that there is no visible physical thing to see. In fact, there is no need to have an eye to see. If Allah wills, one may see with his fingertips while his eyes are shut.

Similarly, the jinn, who don't possess a physical body, can as a force of life, may (or may not) be seen in a particle of an object...

Further, the jinn may also have a physical body of their own. However, just as it is not necessary for us to see everything, it is an obvious fact that we don't see all the particles composing the things that we do see... Therefore, while there are many beings in front of our eyes we may not see them. Just as we don't see microbes with our bare eyes, there may be particles of light in the air that we cannot determine with our senses. Some of these may be close to us, some far, some above us and some below...

We have not discovered all of the physical forces yet. This being the case, both from the spiritual and physical point of view, it is not correct for a human with a rational mind to deny the existence of beings that have been veiled from the human senses."

Feyruz Abadi, another distinguished Islamic scholar, gives us the following summarized information about the **jinn** in his book called **'Basair'** (Wisdom):

'There are two opinions regarding the **jinn**: (Obviously, he is talking in reference to his own time).

1. 'Jinn' is a name given to the invisible spiritual beings that cannot be determined by the human (five) senses. It corresponds to the word **'ins'** (human). Thus, in this context, the word jinn references the angels, the devils and the **jinns.** Therefore, there is a special and a general relation between the angels and the **jinns.**

Every angel is a **jinn;** but a **jinn** is not an angel.

2. **Jinn** is the name given to some of the spiritual (bodiless) beings, as the spiritual beings consist of three groups:

a) The benefic ones, which are the angels.

b) The malefic ones, which are the devils.

c) Those in between who have both benefic and malefic aspects, these are precisely the community of the jinn.[35]

Though we shall explain in more detail later, let us state what the words **'shihab** and **'samum** mean in the Arabic Language since it is closely related to our subject based on the commentary of the late Hamdi Yazır.

In the dictionary, **'shihab** means a **'flame of fire'**.

The meaning of the word **'samm'** derives from **'semm'**, which is poison and it is inherent in the word **'semmum'**. The **'semm'** means poison and **semmilhayah** means **'tiny pores'**. As a matter of fact, the **tiny pores** on our skin from which sweat is secreted and air is taken in are called **'masamma'**, which is the singular form. The plural form is called **masamm** or **masammah**.

The fact that **jann** (or the Jinn) have been created from the **'poisonous fire'** reveals that the jinn and the Satan have the capacity to penetrate into the hidden pores of a human and poison him.[36]

---

[35] *Elmalili,* 'The True Religion'-Volume: 3, Page: 2030
[36] *Elmalili,* 'The True Religion' -Volume: 4, Page: 3059

13

THE STATE OF THE MUSLIMS WHO DENY THE JINN

As can be seen, the Quran covers extensive information on the jinn; what they have done and what they have in plan for humans.

Denying these verses means denying the Quran...

That is, to deny the existence of the jinn is to deny the fact that the Quran is a sacred book revealed by Allah!

Moreover, in **the Religion of Islam,** all scholars who have attained a certain spiritual station are of the common belief that he who denies a single verse in the Quran has denied the entire Quran...

Think of an individual who claims to be a Muslim, who claims to have faith in Allah and His Rasul (saw) and then either directly denies the existence of the jinn or indirectly denies them by misconstruing the verses on the jinn as "microbes"!

Clearly, there is an important reason why such denial would take place. Typically, such individuals are under the effect of the jinn!

If one closely examines the lives of such people, they will see that these individuals are either in connection with or possessed by the jinn.

Some are aware of this connection, and despite this knowing they deliberately insist on their denial because they don't want to reveal their vested interests and the benefits they gain from the jinn.

While others are not even aware that they are possessed by the jinn and ignorantly deny their existence or make absurd interpretations like the "jinn are microbes"...

What is certain is that those who directly or indirectly deny the jinn lack sufficient knowledge of Islam and/or have inadvertently become possessed by the jinn.

14

THE METHODS OF DECEPTION AND POSSESSION OF THE JINN

As previously mentioned, due to their structural advantage the jinn have the ability to make connections with humans and make them submit to their ways.

Many times, however, humans who have become possessed by the jinn either deny this or hide it to save themselves from being ashamed.

For when these connections are revealed they not only feel embarrassed in their communities, but also lead themselves to disaster by taking advice from people who have no knowledge of dealing with the jinn.

As we have stated before, the following verse from the Quran clearly and openly talks about how the jinn take humans under their command and use them like robots:

"The Day when He will gather them together (and say), **"O community of jinn, you have truly possessed** (misled from reality) **the vast majority of mankind."**[37]

The beings called the jinn, the presence of whom humans can't detect with their five senses, enslave humans in two ways:

1. By openly revealing themselves to the person...

---

[37] Quran 6:128

2. Without revealing themselves and not allowing the person to become aware of their presence...

In both cases, they usually make connection under the guise of a religious figure or a religious cause.

That is, they predominantly take advantage of the person's religious and/or humanistic beliefs/ideals and approach them from these angels.

15

HOW THE JINN MAKE 'OPEN' CONTACT WITH HUMANS

This is a type of Jinn-Human relationship whereby the jinn generally force humans into their possession… It is usually women who are prone to this situation.

The **jinn** generally establish this connection, especially with short-tempered nervous women, following birth-giving or during illnesses with high fever or accidents. This is because during such periods, the brain is busy with the extra activity taking place in various parts of the body and the person is thus unable to competently control their brain. As a result, the **jinn** take advantage of this weakness and manipulate that part of the brain. They then appear to the person in whatever form they like and force the person to do whatever they desire.

Sometimes this act of forcing can take place by sending impulses to the pain center of the brain and causing the person to experience pain, and other times, by triggering the center of fear to make the individual feel extremely frightened and hence submissive to their commands.

In any case, they trigger the brain by sending signals to a specific region in the brain at particular intervals to establish their desired effect.

As we shall explain in the following chapters, whenever psychics and mediums go into a trance, they experience exactly the same thing. They are asked to relax and let themselves loose at the onset. Here, the objective is to decrease the control the person has over his brain, thereby preparing the platform for the jinn with whom the contact is planned, so that he can easily take the individual under his possession.

In such scenarios, women have reportedly claimed the jinn who appeared to them was an extremely handsome man.

The jinn who establish such connections with women or young girls usually marry them and engage in sexual activity, during which these women see and feel the jinn with whom they are interacting as a solid, physical person as if it were a human male. However, as the jinn do not have a tangible physical body, inevitably the following question comes to mind:

-How on earth can a jinn who cannot even become completely physical manage to satisfy a woman with a physical human body?

In such conditions, the jinn stimulate the centers in the brain responsible for sexual arousal. All scientists who work in the field of physiology know very well that when an electro shock is applied to a certain center of the brain, it is possible to make a person feel and do whatever you want.

In fact, it is not always a relation between a female human and a male jinn. Sexual relations also take place between female jinn and male humans and homosexuals.

In all of these cases, the common trait is that it is always a member of the **jinn** that forcefully initiate the contact with a human, simply for the purpose of fulfilling their selfish desires. In general, people who have been forced into such positions are mournful about it as these events take place without their conscious consent.

In most of these situations, especially when a connection is made between a human woman and a jinn man, the woman isolates herself from the world around her and retreats into a room…

If the jinn with whom she is in contact is an atheist he prevents her from taking a bath.

On the other hand, however, sometimes the opposite takes place, whereby the woman wants to bath all the time. In extreme cases for example, when the woman is left alone after a sexual intercourse with the jinn, she experiences a state of shock due to the unpleasant situation she's in and stays in the bath washing herself for hours on end.

The field of medicine cannot diagnose these cases; they try to cure the patient by means of electro-shock, which only creates disorder in the brain cells followed by what seems to be a state of calmness. This of course does not mean that the person has been cured, it is merely a temporary reaction to the shock.

Generally, those with a "strong breath" i.e. healing powers, can help cure such cases. I will provide more detail on this in the following chapters…

We had mentioned that there are two ways by which the jinn make open contact…

If the jinn wants to make contact in the manner described above, it is usually established via un-Islamic or 'inferior' ways.

Besides forced relationships, they also make the person live a miserable life in filth and dirt.

In order to easily deceive humans, the first method the jinn prefer is to cut the persons ties to the source of Islamic knowledge, as the most comprehensive knowledge on the jinn is found in Islamic sources.

Once the person is deprived of this knowledge, they become much susceptible giving the jinn a significant advantage over themselves.

Surely one cannot take precaution against something about which they have no knowledge!

The jinn prevent people from acquiring knowledge about them, lest they take precaution!

Abdulkareem al-Jili, a noble saint and the author of 'The Perfect Man' says in the chapter "The possessors of the seven levels of earth" that the jinn who live within the atmosphere of the earth are of seven classes. He says that the weakest among them are the ones who live in the second level of the earth and they influence humans by obstructing their mechanism of contemplation. The most evil ones called "ifrit" (demon) live in the fifth level of the earth (the heavens of the earth consists of seven layers). As for those who live in the sixth and the seventh layers, al-Jili says, no man can have influence over them.

The most evil activity carried out by the jinn within the Islamic societies is leading people astray under the guise of the Truth (haqq).

This can take place in a few ways…

The most basic was is fortune telling and dealing with black magic disguised under a religious title such as "*hodja*" …

Those who enter a relation with the jinn via marriage or by some other means can give information from the past by using their jinn partner, and also provide clues about the future, commonly based on guesswork and probability.

Most of what they prophesize for the future are inaccurate and don't effectuate. There is no place for fortune telling and black magic in the religion of Islam, it is a great offence and a huge responsibility! It is considered among the great sins!

Unfortunately, today so many people are squandering away their lives in the futile pursuit of false masters, who are deluded by the jinn.

There are many alleged mahdis (messiah) and masters, a few in almost every city, who lead so many people astray based on misguiding inspirations they receive from the jinn.

Sufism, before anything, is a battle against one's self! Hence why the Rasul of Allah (saw) said, "We are returning from the small battle to the big battle" on their way home after gaining victory from a great battle.

This being the case, so many "Sufis" and their "great saints" can't even stop smoking!

If one cannot battle with his ego against a simple addiction, how can he overcome other greater challenges and become a saint?

As many sources all commonly agree, the food of the jinn are scents.

Their favorite scent is that of tobacco smoke…

When they find someone who smokes cigarettes, they will not easily leave that person alone. The jinn are the greatest contributors to the increase in cigarette addiction.

When they find someone who smokes, they send a signal to their brain making the person feel stressed which leads him to light up a cigarette. Shortly after he takes a few puffs the person starts to be feel relieved. For his jinn acquaintance has taken his nutrition and stopped sending that signal. Hence the person finishes his cigarettes and feels relieved.

After some time when the jinn needs more nutrition he sends the signal again and the person lights up again… and on goes the cycle…

If you encounter a "hodja" or a "master" who constantly smokes recite the following verses from the Quran:

Chapter as-Sad Verse 41, chapter al-Muminun Verses 98-99 and chapter as-Saffat verse 7.

You will see that the waves you send by reciting these verses will begin to repel the jinn that works through the "hodja" and rupture their connection causing the hodja to act and speak in an unstable irrational way.

Moreover, if you recite these verses near fortune tellers, psychics, and mediums you will see the effects for yourself. Here is the transliteration of these verses:

"Rabbi inni massaniyyash shaytanu Bi noosbin wa adhab; Rabbi audhu Bika min hamazatish shayateen wa audhu bika Rabbi an yahduroon. Wa hifzan min qulli shaytanin mareed."[38]

The saints of Allah never smoke! This is validated in Sayyid Abdulaziz Ad-Dabbagh's book "Al Ibriz" (Pure Gold) written centuries ago, who also notes the People of the Diwan (The Supreme Council of Saints) never ever smoked.

It is a noteworthy observation that while the Rijal al-Ghayb (the Men of the Unknown) never smoked, almost all of those who are in connection with the jinn are serious smoke addicts.

Hence the biggest and most effective precaution to take to keep the jinn away is to refrain from smoking…

Also, to validate the authenticity of those who are allegedly at a particular spiritual rank, one may check their approach to the following two topics:

1. ONENESS & UNITY (wahdah)

2. FATE

---

[38] Quran 38:41 – 23:97-98 – 37:7

Both those who are unconsciously possessed by the jinn and claim to be a saint out of delusion and those who are consciously in a relationship with the jinn will intentionally refrain from discussing these topics, in order to hide the intellectual incapacity of the jinn ruling them.

The jinn and those under their ruling will always try to keep others away from acquiring knowledge on these two topics, particularly from Sufism, which aims to teach these realities, diverting their attention to everything besides these two topics.

Whenever and where ever you encounter someone who tries to keep you away from learning more about oneness and fate, search for other signs and traces of the jinn before continuing your relationship with them.

The primary reason for this is because the jinn are aware of their inadequacy regarding these realities and hence don't want their fraud to be revealed, and secondly because once a person understands these realities they can be freed of the "god" they have created in their minds and discern the reality of the Oneness of Allah... Obviously the jinn don't want this as **Iblis (Satan), the ancestor of the jinn, has promised to lead the whole of humanity away from Allah!**

The most common way the jinn work against humans is by encouraging them to engage in activities that will deprive them of the life energy (Nur) they will need in the afterlife.

As for the Sufis, the jinn distract them by making them get caught up in intricate details instead of the essence of the reality.

Good morals, abstinence from misdeeds, and worship are the matters of Sufism not of Shariah!

If one spends a lot of time with the matters of shariah in a Sufi gathering then he has not yet started his Sufi journey.

Sufism, begins with practices that enable reaching the secret of unity, which is based on the reality of shariah.

On the other hand, there are also jinn who are Muslims...

They provide simple religious information to the person... Most of which may be correct... This sort of scenario is commonly seen in regions or households that lack religious knowledge.

However, in both of the cases above, those who make contact with the jinn usually refrain from disclosing their situation because most people know nothing about the jinn and/or make fun of them, hence making it difficult to determine such cases.

Contrary to these unusual events, the most common type of human-jinn relation is the one in which the jinn establish connections with people without making themselves be known.

Let us now examine how the jinn do this…

16

HOW THE JINN CONTROL HUMANS WITHOUT THEIR KNOWLEDGE

As previously mentioned, there are two ways in which the jinn rule humans:

a) By taking advantage of the religion of Islam...

b) By diverting humans to humanistic causes...

The most obvious difference between these two is that the first does not accept the concept of reincarnation whereas the second one does...

I will cover the topic on reincarnation in detail in the following chapters so I won't go into detail here other than for the purpose of clarifying our current topic.

Let us first examine how they exploit Islam to rule over people...

This too takes place in two ways:

1. By not letting themselves be known at all
2. Letting themselves be known under a different name and form

First, let us take a look at how they can possess and rule people without revealing themselves...

The most common trait of those who fall under this category is that they have no idea of their connection with the jinn. They simply assume that all the extraordinary experiences they have are the result of their own superior qualities. Due to this they spend their lives looking down upon others, showing fake modesty when necessary.

In one of his books *Muhyiddin Ibn Arabi* states that the most important characteristics of such people is that even though they do not have sufficient knowledge or own any valuable works, they belittle others and constantly assert their superiority.

In addition to this, the second most prominent characteristic of these people is that they do not accept the existence of the jinn, claiming "There is no such thing as jinn, the jinn are simply microbes" …

Paradoxically, they make such claims due to the ideas imposed upon them by the very jinn they deny!

This is a smart tactic applied by the jinn so as to prevent people from questioning their state and eventually finding out about the existence of the jinn, for this would indeed be disadvantageous for them!

Purely for this reason all those who are possessed by the jinn deny their existence based on absurd explanations.

So how do the jinn manage to possess these people?

Such deception generally takes place by someone going into trance and a jinn claiming through them, "I am the spirit of Rumi!" or "I am such and such master/sheikh/guru" or the pen starts to write by itself "I am such and such great person" etc.

Sometimes the jinn actually takes the form of that person and becomes visible in their appearance. There are other ways but these are the most common.

For example, the person in trance says, "I am the spirit of Rumi" and salutes the people there and then starts talking in a sophisticated language.

When examined one may see that the speech really is different than the usual speech capacity of the person in trance… Hence, ignorant of the existence of the jinn, the people there automatically believe that they are actually in contact with Rumi or the spirit of some great saint!

Considering the fact that the majority of the people in today's world have no knowledge on the jinn, and the attractiveness of hidden/mysterious phenomenon, it becomes pretty believable…

Think of someone who goes into a trance in front of you and then starts saying things that have absolutely no coherence to how this person acts and talks in normal life, and to top it off, they say things about you and your past that only you know about!

Hence, slowly but surely the people witnessing this start believing that they are actually in contact with a great saint.... All of these people usually have a common trait. Generally, they are all sincere, devout people with good intentions who are sad about not being able to fulfill the requisites of their religious belief and who are looking for ways of salvation, but who on the other hand, have close to no religious knowledge…

Eventually this 'being' starts to appear in the dreams of the people that gather around him and starts to reveal some of their private issues, further strengthening their tie to him through emotional exploitation…

In time he tells the people that no "revitalizer" (mujaddid) is expected to come and that people are going to receive guidance through channels like this…and then guides the people to do certain things…

He tells them to pray, give alms, fast, engage in good deeds and abstain from the bad, hence triggering their humanistic qualities and fortifying their connection… This is the first stage!

In the second stage however, he puts forward his devilish act. He starts imposing distorted information, things that can only be understood by those who have solid religious knowledge. And this is where the real game starts.

He makes some people believe in the concept of **Wahdat-al-Wujud** (Unity of Existence)! However, what he really guides to under this label is not the true understanding of the oneness of the existence, but rather **'PANTHEISM'**. It has nothing to do with the Unity of the Existence! By doing so, he makes them believe that they themselves are *'Allah'*.

Or, he wrongly narrates quotes and gives examples from Rumi, or other popular saints and scholars, to assert the concept of reincarnation; the belief of coming back to the world after death in another body…

Hence, he starts misguiding people to incorrect beliefs.

The truth is, anybody with proper religious knowledge observing them closely can easily detect all the details that go against Islam. On the other hand, deceiving by using a pencil is a much more simple method than what we have already described above.

With this method, the individual never sees the being that is in contact with him.

He simply holds the pencil on a paper and the pencil starts to write by itself.

At first, the being uses a nickname, for example he makes the pencil write:

'I am Mawlana Jalaluddin Rumi! You, the blessed person, the traveler embarking on the sacred road to Allah, I salute you!'

This astonishes the individual who is doing the act of writing, the being then continues until eventually the pencil gets used to writing all by itself!

The pencil writes that whoever is holding it is a noble person, one of the leading saints of that time, and provides lots of convincing evidence that he is actually a saint.

The being carries on with the act of writing, giving answers to the questions crossing the individual's mind.

In the beginning, the person does not know what the pencil will write. However, when he starts to pay more attention, he realizes that before the pencil actually writes anything down, the words and the short sentences first come to his mind.

Following this, the jinn with a nickname makes him write poems, books and starts telling him about the activities carried out by various people in the past. Meanwhile, in order to gain the confidence of the individual, the jinn makes some predictions for the future.

Let us give an example to illustrate this point:

Couple of years ago in Ankara, a jinn came to a meeting where a group of people were present and he introduced himself as:

'The angel named Basheer-al Kiraam!'

He then made some future predictions, summarized as follows:

"The starting date of the third world war will be around the years 1974-75 at which time Israel will defeat the Arabs and expand its lands reaching the Turkish borders. Turkey will manage to survive the third world war with very few losses and around the year 1980, a person named *Mahdi* will appear in Turkey. According to this claim, the expected *Mahdi* will be someone who has reached the age of 50 with no special qualities and that he will be speaking through the mouth of an angel."

We have already mentioned that by appearing in the image of the saints and then becoming visible to the individual in that form, the jinn can deceive that individual and tie him to themselves.

Generally speaking, the individuals whom they deceive in this way are completely devoid of true religious knowledge.

The person who is confronted with such a scene gets shocked at first. He has no other choice but to believe in the person in front of him who is dressed up in clothes resembling those of the olden days, wearing a gown and a turban. Helplessly, he believes!

From then on, he starts doing whatever the jinn tells him to do. With all the things he hears and relays from that "being" he manages to gather a lot of people around him. However, the people around him cannot actually see what he can see. For this reason, they have to believe whatever he tells them. Eventually, some of those who are gathered around him start seeing that being in their dreams.

Besides, from time to time the individual who is possessed by the jinn could actually show that being to his most loyal followers and thus form a group whose members are strongly attached to him.

Meanwhile, the jinn will appear to that individual in different types of clothing and lead the person to believe he is making contact with different saints because he has been 'enlightened'. On the other hand, sometimes the person may make his jinn appear as noble saints to his friends to fortify their attachment through deception.

As a matter of fact, some individuals who have been obsessed by a very strong jinn can make a number of jinn dressed as saints appear to the people around him, making them think he is an extremely important person for all these saints to be visiting him.

This situation can go to such extents that in some cases, the person who is not fully aware that he is possessed and who thinks of himself as a very important person due to the ideas imposed upon him by the jinn, actually thinks he is permitting other saints into his presence, whereby a door will open in the room, and two or three jinn dressed in old clothes will enter in the guise of very well-known saints of the past.

You can imagine the awe and fascination of those witnessing this scene. There is no way for them to know whether who they are seeing are saints or jinn! They are simply shocked!

From that moment onwards, they are powerfully and loyally attached to that person as if he is a God.

However, as we already pointed out before, whoever you meet among them, their common characteristic would always be to deny the existence of the jinn.

The jinn that can possess humans can either be an ordinary type or it may be one of their superior ones such as their leaders. It may also be one of those who are well known in their group.

A jinn generally chooses a teenager with a high brain capacity for communication skills and puts him among others who are already possessed by him! This generally occurs in people who are between the ages of 15-24. In some cases, however, it can take place at much younger ages.

As soon as the choice has been made and the subject to be possessed is determined by the jinn, the next step is to attach the person to himself completely.

To be able to achieve this, the jinn disguises himself as a well-known, respectable religious figure and goes into his dream, only to impose on the individual the idea that he is going to be a great, important person.

The person that the jinn disguises himself under could either be 'Hazrat Khalid' or 'Mawlana Jalaladdin Rumi' or 'Muhyiddin Ibn Arabi' or any other saint who is well known in the society.

As a result of all these visions that are being shown to the individual, gradually this young person, whether male or female, believes that s/he really is going to be a very great person.

Sometimes s/he wants to have something and their wish is immediately granted by jinn.

He thinks that Allah has made his wish come true; unaware that it is the play of his **jinn**.

When he has to sit an exam, for example, he is assisted in the examination.

When he talks to someone, he gains superiority over the other person owing to the pressure that the jinn exerts on him. It seems as though others simply cannot resist him.

As such, he starts to improve and grow by the day.

As time goes on, he feels more and more changes in his condition. He is also informed of certain minor events that are to take place in the near future. If he is unaware of his connection with the jinn, he assumes that all these incidents take place by the faculty of his sixth sense. He may have instant knowledge about a particular event which might occur in another place at the same moment.

He makes a request to solve somebody's problem, for example, and that demand is immediately granted by his jinn. Because he assumes himself as a great man, he thinks his request is actually being granted by the help of Allah as he is a man with great wisdom.

In the end, he claims that he has finally become an expert; a man with a great intellect in a certain field. He thinks that he no longer needs anybody else! He sees himself more superior than others! From this point on, he simply acts in accordance with the inspirations that he senses within himself.

If his profession is in the field of theology for instance, he claims to be the greatest religious man in this field.

If he has his own business, he spreads around the idea that he is the greatest saint of his time, namely the Qutub-ul-Aqtaab (Highest Ranking Saint).

He may cure hopeless ailments and diseases by using very simple medications; he may also make a diagnosis that could not be made, or make the paralyzed move and walk!

Whatever his profession may be, he may display extraordinary activities, as a result of which, he may easily become very famous and gather thousands of followers around himself.

Of course, those who have extensive knowledge on these matters can easily discern the reality of the situation. However, those who do not believe in such things may accuse him of being a charlatan, a magician or as someone dealing with witchcraft. On the contrary, those who believe in him will treat him as the greatest saint or even consider him to be at the same level as the Mahdi (The Messiah) or as Jesus (pbuh).

Doubtlessly, at this point, the greatest pleasure and joy belongs to the jinn who has successfully managed to secure his subject.

For now, through the jinn of that individual, thousands of others have been connected to the assembly of the **jinn,** and they can do whatever they want to those people. Therefore, in order to strengthen the position of that certain individual, they can even access the dreams of some people for the purpose of establishing close relations with that person and suggest them to help him.

At the same time, they can provide religious information to that particular individual and present him as a great religious man. So, those who are not aware of this choose him as a religious leader for themselves.

From now on, that person starts to spread around fatwa (religious rulings) without making any reference to Islamic sources. He gives his verdict on some of the permissible (halal) things in Islam as if they were prohibited (haram). Furthermore, he starts to impose these ideas upon others in such a way so as to make others believe that he is a leader who is bringing along new rulings which are suitable to that time period.

As a result, the individual eventually gathers a lot of people around him and starts to live as if he were a reformer of religion (mujaddid) and an Islamic scholar. Meanwhile, the jinn who has possessed him establishes his supremacy over him! This jinn who has been successful in doing this is honored among his kind and his competitors.

Even though there are such examples in Turkey, we are not going to place an emphasis on them here and instead we will illustrate the point we have mentioned above by an example and taking some sections from Ahmad Qadian's life.

The best example on the face of this planet confirming what we have mentioned above is from Ahmad Qadiani who established the Qadian sect and who lived his life in connection with the jinn. According to his life story, which he himself has written, he was born in a town called Qadian in India.

He learned that his family originated from Samarkand by means of unveiling (*Kashf*). In terms of his character, he was a sensitive person who isolated himself from others and preferred to remain in seclusion.

From time to time, he would stay alone by himself to perform certain practices to discover the true meaning of his origin or 'self'.

According to his narration, on one particular day, he suddenly hears a mysterious voice; a kind of voice which could only be heard by him.

This mysterious voice informs him that his father will die on that very day after the call for the evening prayer.

Upon hearing this, he becomes extremely frightened and feels very sad. Amidst this fear and sorrow the voice comes again: *'Is Allah not sufficient for His servant?'* And his father really dies late that afternoon.

Ahmad Qadiani explains as follows:

"Afterwards, I've heard that voice many more times. It was that voice which taught me many things! It introduced me to the world and made me famous! As I was poor and in need, that voice provided me with plenty of richness so that I could perform good deeds help those in a charitable way!"

In time the jinn would establish a secure connection with Ahmad Qadian and eventually direct him towards some wrong beliefs, but for the most part he is convinced that he is being guided by the divine:

"I have no doubt that the voices that came to my ears are of a divine nature. Because, if I had been fooled by the Satan the evilness in me would have become manifest, which I would have definitely noticed. Sometimes I could hear words from afar while at other times the words came out of my own mouth, but I was not the one who said them.

This happened to such an extent that sometimes I could even speak in different languages of which I had no prior knowledge.

I do not believe that an ordinary spirit or spirits possessed me by entering inside of me.

This is something quite different! But in what way is it different? All I know is that it feels different and this is enough for me and those who are connected to me!"

Finally, he comes out one day and claims:

'LA ILAHA ILLALLAH, MUHAMMADAN RASULULLAH! (There is no god only Allah, Muhammad is the Rasul of Allah) I am the Messiah, the son of Mary who fills the heart of Muhammad with his love, the last and greatest of all the Rasuls.

No other Rasul or Nabi other than Muhammad will come, but only one individual will have the privilege to attain his honorable rank. That individual is me! Ahmad of Qadian has become a Nabi (Messenger) without causing any harm to his master Muhammad whose rank is "Khatam-ul- Nabi" (Seal of the Nabis) and he has received a sacred duty from Allah!"

Mirza Ghulam Ahmad of Qadian died after the First World War. He manifested a lot of signs, which were referred to as miracles.

Thousands of people got connected to him by their dreams. Those who stayed close to him for a period of forty days received divine signs and cleared themselves from all their denials. He was able to cure the paralyzed by a few strokes of the hand and the ill simply by saying a few words. These are some of his so-called miracles, which occurred on a regular basis. Moreover, some people who refused to accept him and who argued with him eventually ended up dying, which made his fame spread even more.

Mirza Ghulam Ahmad of Qadian claimed that he was the Mahdi (the Messiah) and said that Jesus (pbuh) who is expected to return to the world in the last era and the Mahdi were the same person. In the end, he claimed to be this particular individual. If we examine this event more realistically, it can be seen that he did this in order to spread Islam. There is no wonder that in doing so, he was successful to a certain extent. However, when the matter is examined in depth, it could be seen that the jinn who initially managed to make a single person dependent on them, used that person again, so that thousands of other individuals also became dependent on them through that person. In order to achieve this task more efficiently, they used Islam as a tool.

As Muhyiddin Ibn Arabi states in his book 'Futuhut al-Makkiyya' (Meccan Revelations), the most significant feature that is observed on the people who have been possessed by the jinn is an accented ego and 'pride'.

In general, such people consider themselves to be the most superior person of their times. In fact, they even claim to be the most important and high ranked religious person to come after Muhammad (saw), the final Nabi.

According to a group of the Islamic society, *'Mahdi'* is the name given to the religious leader who is expected to appear in the world one or two hundred years before the actual doomsday, and who is expected to possess extraordinary powers and cause Islam to spread all over the world!

The jinn have misguided many individuals into thinking they are the awaited *'Mahdi'*, who in turn deceived many people in their surroundings.

Let us now examine how the jinn deceive individuals by channeling them towards humanistic goals in the name of "spiritualism."

A new trend started to become popular in Turkey as of the 1940's called spiritualism. Although it was Dr. Bedri Ruhselman who made it widespread, it was actually Garbis Fikri, the owner of the Gayret Library who initially introduced the subject to Turkey.

In the introduction section of Garbis Fikri's "Encyclopedia of Spiritualism" it says:

"It was 37 years ago from today that I published a two-volume book in our country for the first time, named 'Communicating with the Jinn - Spiritualism - Faqirism – Magnetism' as well as a magazine titled 'Spiritualism' comprised of 15 fascicules which had a remarkable impact on the society.

Recently, I have published the 3-volume book 'The Spirit and the Universe' written by Bedri Ruhselman. Following this, I have published another book from Bedri Ruhselman called 'Among the Spirits'. Last of all, I have published 'The Encyclopedia of the Spirit' prepared by Dr. Sevil AKAY and Ishak Lütfi Kuday, which was the outcome of a long research giving extensive information about all the branches of Spiritualism.'

So, this is how the movement of **'Communicating with the Spirits'** in Turkey started.

However, as Garbis Fikri of Armenian origin states, at the beginning this event was known as **'Communicating with the Jinn'.** In time it was disguised and presented to the people as **'Communicating with the**

Spirits'. After the 1960's, it was changed to **'Making contact with Extraterrestrials'**.

In order to dominate people who either have no connection to the religion of Islam or who are Muslim only in label and are far from practicing the requisites of Islam, the jinn take advantage of humanistic ideas.

They present various rules and rituals to reach the state of a 'perfect human' and invite all humans to this state.

In this manner, the jinn manage to gather many humans around themselves and spread out many humanistic ideas.

In such meetings, a person is usually hypnotized and put to sleep, or in other words goes into a state of trance and makes a connection with a 'spirit'.

A group of people come together in a room, the lights are dimmed and a blue or red light with a low voltage is used.

Then, a person who has psychic qualities is put into a trance mode by the suggestions made by the group.

In reality, this activity is carried out solely for the purpose of making the subject sleep so that the effect of the 'human consciousness' over the body can be completely lifted and made ineffective.

The individual who has been put to sleep then starts saying things like:

"I'm gradually rising higher and higher... I am now passing through the clouds... I've now started to see such and such things in front of me..."

Then, he starts to talk with those entities that he is seeing. Following this, those that he is seeing ask for permission to talk. In this manner, the conversation with the spirit of so and so person begins.

However, all of this is nothing other than a game put on stage by the jinn who is already in direct contact with the people that are present there. In reality, the person who has been put into a state of trance and is sleeping has not even moved a millimeter from where he was when he slept.

As for what is really taking place behind the scenes:

Soon after that person goes to sleep, in other words the human consciousness dominating the 'brain' and the 'physical body' becomes inactive, the jinn whose frequency is the closest to the frequency of the person sleeping takes over the scene and makes contact with the individual.

At the onset, this jinn sends signals to the brain of the person whose acting as an adaptor to influence the section in the brain that is connected to speech. As a result, the jinn is able to address the people there from within the mouth of that person.

Since the people there can't see anything, they think the claims of the sleeping person such as "I'm going to that place, I'm talking to that person" are in fact true.

In reality, nobody has gone anywhere!

On one hand, there is a human being who is put to deep sleep and is thus unable to control his conscious mind and on the other hand, there is a jinn who has taken control of the brain of the this individual to deceive the people there.

From this point on the effect of the game depends on the strength and capacity of the jinn.

If the jinn is a clever one, he can take this opportunity to easily influence and possess the people there.

Inadvertently, the people who are present there will do whatever the jinn tells them to, because there is a being who is communicating with them by addressing each one of them with their innermost secrets, yet this being cannot be seen! Clearly, for those witnessing, denying this "seeming reality" would be complete foolishness because they are not aware of the reality of what is really taking place!

17

ON THE MAHDI & MAHDISM

Based on some of the explanations of Muhammad (saw), the spiritually guided ones and those who belong to the religion of Islam believe that Allah sends a reviver of religion (mujaddid), whose task is to spread the religion of Islam, every century.

The duty of this person, based on the explanations of the Rasul of Allah (saw) is to explain the religion of Islam according to the understanding of the present time, to show the people that religion is not something pertaining to the past, and to guide them to the reality.

The only direct descendant of the Rasul of Allah (saw) whose name was Mahdi, his twelfth grandson, fell into a well and died of drowning at the age of six. The awaited Mahdi has nothing to do with this person.

"Mahdi" is the nickname of the awaited one...

In some of his explanations, the Rasul of Allah (saw) says "A reviver carrying my name will come in the future who will..." Some commentators interpreted this assertion as though the actual name of the person will either be 'Ahmed' or 'Muhammad'. As a matter of fact, Mirza Ghulam Ahmad of Qadian thought that he was the Mahdi himself, because his name was 'Ahmed' and he was manipulated by the jinn.

There is extensive information on this subject in the hadith collection called 'Ibn Majah.

Imam Al-Rabbani Ahmad Farooq Sirhindi is a very well-known character among the Sufis who became famous as the reviver of the year 2000 according to the Islamic calendar. In his book named *Maktubat* (The

Letters), he gives us the following information about the rank of the 'Mahdi':

"The Rabb of the Mahdi of whose coming we have been informed is the attribute of knowledge.

Like Hadhrat Ali (ra), this noble person too is connected to Jesus (pbuh).

It is almost as though one foot of Jesus (pbuh) is on the head of Hadhrat Ali (ra) and the other foot is on the head of the Mahdi."

In the Encyclopedia of Islam, the following information is given in regards to the expected person referred to as *Mahdi*:

"The meaning of Mahdi is a person who is divinely guided by Allah. This word was used in the past, both to refer to certain individuals in the past and in reference to one particular individual who is expected to arrive before the doomsday.

This word was used for the first time to refer to the caliph of the state of the Amawis, Omar the second, who was known as the 'Mujaddid' (Reviver) and accepted as an honorable figure, blessed with the guidance of Allah.

In later years, however, Omar the second was accepted to be the first Mujaddid (Reviver) and the 7th (and final) would either be 'Mahdi' or 'Jesus' based on two different views."

In his book called 'Muqaddima' (Introduction), Ibn Khaldun states the following about the person referred as the 'Mahdi' in the section titled 'The descendants of Fatima, the position people take concerning her, and the clarification of this matter'

"Know that it has been commonly accepted among the people of Islam throughout the ages that there must be at the end of time the appearance of a man from the lineage of the Rasul of Allah (saw) who will help the religion and bring justice and whom the Muslims will follow and who will gain control over the Islamic lands, and who will be called the Mahdi.

As for his ruling over the world, this will take place with the descension of Jesus (pbuh).

After this the other signs of the Doomsday will transpire and the advent of the Dajjal (Antichrist) will take place.

Jesus (pbuh) will descend after the appearance of the Dajjal (Antichrist) and will kill the Dajjal who will emerge soon after the appearance of the Mahdi."

In his book 'Muqaddima' (Introduction), Ibn Khaldun recounts twenty-four hadith in detail regarding the Mahdi, including six different versions, and questions their authenticity. In 14 of these hadith the Reviver (Mujaddid) is referred to as the 'Mahdi'.

The discussions that are held and debated over the issue of 'Mahdi' within the Islamic community have continued in this manner.

Similarly, it is a common belief in the Islamic world that the Doomsday is going to take place before the year 1600 according to Islamic calendar. This is being derived from the answer given to the following question that was asked to Muhammad (saw): "O *Rasul* of *Allah (saw)*, when will the Doomsday take place?" The Rasul of Allah (saw) answers, "If my community does well, it will be after the year 1000!"

Likewise, the expression that is commonly used among the public that the day of resurrection will not take place before 1500 or after 1600 is purely based on this hadith.

As the figure 2000 is not mentioned, the commentators have construed that the doomsday will take place between the years 1000 and 2000, which by an approximate calculation coincides somewhere between the years 1400 and 1600 according to the Islamic calendar.

Taking into account the fact that in every 200 years a new *Mujaddid* (Reviver) is expected, some Muslims calculated that the final and the 7th *Mujaddid* will arrive around the beginning of the year 1400, and since he will be the final *Mujaddid* he will be called the *'Mahdi'*.

Again, the same people assert that the person who will be called the *'Mahdi'* will also be a saint of the highest rank. He will be able to observe any point in the world at any moment he wishes, and have enough power to rule wherever he wants, whenever he wants. He will remove the blasphemy from the Islamic world and together with Jesus (pbuh) who will descend after the Mahdi, he will teach and spread Islam all over the world, abolishing all the sects and madhaps. He will also enliven the system of belief that was prevalent during the time of the Rasul of Allah (saw).

Many people who lived in various times and places claimed, either explicitly or implicitly, that they were indeed the *Mahdi, and this is still the case* today. Such people easily deceive the people around them taking advantage of their lack of knowledge. Most of them are ruled by the jinn, albeit they are mostly unaware of it. They believe they are the mahdi because of the delusion the jinn cause them through the dreams they see and the visions or epiphanies they receive!

As far as I know, the only way to be exempt from the influence of these people who delude many people through the support of the jinn is by having knowledge and reciting the "prayer of jinn."

There is no definite evidence for the exact date the Mahdi will appear, though for the Muslims his arrival can be any moment. Even the saints, with the exception of those in the **'SUPREME COUNCIL OF SAINTS'** have no knowledge on this matter.

As we get closer to seventeen past the year 1400, according to the Islamic calendar, this topic has become more popular and resultantly, there has been a significant increase in the number of people who claim to be the *Mahdi*.

It's a pity to see so many people who think they are the Mahdi due to their insufficient knowledge and the misguidance of the jinn, leading many others astray and becoming a source of amusement for the jinn.

Based on the teachings of the Rasul of Allah (saw) the real 'Mahdi' will first emerge in Mecca and then move to Medina, upon which an army will be sent against him and this army will be plunged under the earth. These events will serve as evidence that he is indeed the Mahdi.

No sound person living in Istanbul or in Ankara or some other city will claim to be the Mahdi. If he does, then the situation must either be psychiatric or one that needs to be turned over to experts who expel jinn.

As for my own thoughts...

I believe we need to leave it to time; wait and see what happens. For we have seen every year, for twenty years now, how during the pilgrimage (hajj) period people claim "the Mahdi will appear this year" and plan their entire future based on this expectation only to be disappointed.

Despite all of this, we neither deny it, which is the output of impotence and limited comprehension, nor confirm it, as this matter isn't associated with the pillars of faith and there is no concrete evidence regarding its accuracy. If such a person does appear and we meet him, we will make our final decision then, and act accordingly.

Indeed, time answers and explains everything in the best way!

On the other hand, there has been a significant increase in the number of people claiming to be the Mahdi. Almost in every city there is a few people who not only delude themselves but also those around them. It's even sadder that these naive yet ignorant people have given rein to the jinn who is ruling behind the scenes. And it is very difficult to be freed from it!

Some of these people are exaggerated by the media, while others wait in silence for the day they will rise to glory!

I have already explained the reason behind these super mahdis who think they are the sheikh of tens of thousands is that they are possessed by the jinn.

Now let us talk about the other aspect...

If you're searching for a particular channel on your TV, you will encounter the following situation.

At first, your screen will be covered with unclear, unknown, distorted images, as you get closer to the broadcast you are searching for the disturbances will begin to disappear until finally you see a net, clear broadcast!

As I previously explained, every single event that transpires in the world, does so through the various cosmic influences, stage by stage. Everything starts from the bottom, from zero-state, rises in stages until it reaches its highest point, and then it starts to go down back to zero again! This is the absolute order and mechanism of the system!

In this world, all events are formed in certain cycles and in the light of today's terminology, at certain periods, certain trends become **"fashionable"**.

For the past perhaps twenty years or so, my answer to those who claimed *the Mahdi will arrive that year*, has been a solid 'No.' By divine grace, I was never mistaken. For my research on this topic indicated the arrival of the Mahdi was still quite a long time away.

But why did so many people who have not even discerned the meaning of 'Amantu' were delusively claiming to be the Mahdi?

There were two main reasons for this.

First, because they were unaware, they were being ruled by the jinn and were inadvertently being dragged into a situation against which they could not take precaution, misleading many others alongside.

Secondly, they were under the influence of the disturbed energy waves rather than clear original ones.

The disturbed unclear energy waves carrying the meaning and wisdom of the Mahdi, or in other words, the pre-runners of the Mahdi, have already begun to spread on Earth.

The same goes for the Messiah!

For this reason, in the years to come, many individuals will appear under the guise of the 'Mahdi' or 'JESUS' and unfortunately, they will deceive many people.

Therefore, to be protected from such delusion and to have a more realistic point of view one must know the facts with certainty.

Starting with **hadith** books such as *'Qutub-u Sitte'* many books and works unanimously agree that Jesus (pbuh) will come back to Earth. And this claim was made by Jesus (pbuh) himself, at that time, for 2000 years later.

Be cautious!

If Jesus (pbuh) said he'd come back 2000 years later and he said this before he died, then he would have said this when he was 33, i.e. the year 33 based on the Gregorian calendar, which indicates his return will be in year 2033.

Before the return of Jesus (pbuh) to earth, the Antichrist (Dajjal) will emerge and he will manifest extraordinary powers causing great provocation and disorder to mankind. He will claim to be 'God' who has descended from the heavens and that he is the long-awaited Rabb of the humans.

The dajjal will remain on earth for forty days and at the end of this period, Jesus (saw) will return to earth and kill him.

Jesus (saw) will live on earth for 40 years, 9 to 11 of these years he will spend with the Mahdi. That is, the Mahdi, who will have already emerged before Jesus (pbuh), will spend the last 9-11 years of his life with Jesus (pbuh) after which he will pass on to the afterlife.

The Dajjal will appear 9-11 years before the Mahdi passes away.

My late master, Haji Osman Efendy (also known as the Madinian) told me the following in 1963:

"The Egyptian astrologers had written in the newspapers of Cairo some years ago that the star of Mahdi is born… He is here now, growing up among us…"

With respect to all this information and the things I'm unable to pen here, my personal opinion is:

Before the advent of Mahdi, the third world war will take place and Europe will be razed to the ground. After this the Mahdi will reveal himself during a pilgrimage season due to the persistence of the Rijal al-Ghayb (The Men of the Unknown). Following this, he will go to Medina and there, an army would be sent onto him from Damascus and this army will be swallowed by the earth and plunged under the ground completely somewhere around near Medina. It is also mentioned in various valuable sources that the Dajjal (Antichrist) will emerge while the *Mahdi* is in **Istanbul**…

Therefore, there is strong implications that there will be lots of political changes and wars in Europe, the United States, Russia and the Middle East before the Mahdi appears.

In short, whatever the case may be, the start of these events would be no sooner than the beginning of the 2000's.

Considering the astrological transits, there is a strong indication that important events will transpire after the planet Uranus goes into the sign of Aquarius in 1996. If we also take into consideration the fact that Pluto will enter Sagittarius approximately around the same period, the experts can clearly see the kind of important events are awaiting us…

So, as this period comes closer, the number of people claiming to be the *Mahdi* or *Jesus* will increase and this will also cause the emergence of false *Dajjals*.

According to an explanation given by Muhammad (saw), before the arrival of the actual *Dajjal* close to 30 false *Dajjals* will emerge and they will all claim to be a 'prophet.''

This simply indicates that before and after every 'original' broadcast, false side waves will always appear.

As a result of their incorrect belief in a god in space or their ignorant assumption that Allah is a god in the heavens, many people will fall into the the trap of accepting the dajjal as their god.

The only way people can protect themselves from the dajjal is by understanding Allah as explained by Muhammad (saw).

Those who have not discerned Allah, as defined and explained by the Quran, are vulnerable to becoming the victims of a false "god."

On the other hand, I would like to take this opportunity to mention another important point, while we're on the topic.

There are indeed some people who have absolutely no relation with the jinn, who are students of great masters and under their protection, but who also think they may be the Mahdi… So how can it be that even though they are under the protection of saints and have no relation with the jinn that these people also assume to be the Mahdi and give this impression to their surroundings?

In Sufism, as the aspirant continues on his path, he encounters certain states. For example, the "Rank of Gaws" the "Rank of Hızır", the "Rank of Mahdi" etc...

The Sufis know, as the aspirant advances through these spiritual stations, the qualities of that particular rank is reflected on him like a mirror reflecting the rays of the Sun, the individual inadvertently starts to think of himself as the source of that light...

Such people may not be able to refrain themselves from this pleasure and remain in that state for a considerable length of time. As a result, they begin to think of themselves as the actual saint to whom that rank and state really belongs... Similarly, those around him who have not become fully enlightened also assume that he is the actual person through whose rank he is simply transiting.

If his master is powerful enough, the aspirant may be saved from this state easily and will see the reality. But if his master is not strong enough, if he has not yet reached perfection, then he may stay in that state for 5-10 years, sometimes his entire life, and resultantly believe he is the actual person of that rank, deceiving not only himself but also those around him.

18

ON THE ANTICHRIST

When we hear the word 'antichrist' we automatically think of the creature called 'dajjal' mentioned in the religion of Islam and other religions.

According to the information conveyed to us, the creature named 'dajjal' will display extraordinary, supernatural things to humans, and eventually seduce them into believing in him...

However, according to Islamic sources, close to thirty false dajjals will appear before the actual dajjal and claim to be a prophet, ordering the people to do certain things while forbidding them from other things.

The final and actual dajjal will claim to be Allah and ask the people to worship him, he will also display some extraordinary powers.

This is why inevitably, what comes to mind first is the thirty or so false dajjals that are expected to appear before the real one...

Because whether in Turkey or various other places in the world, the jinn delude the masses in the name of humanistic goals, and present either themselves or one of the leaders of their group as a modern prophet. This prophet then orders the people to do certain things and promises them that they will be leaders in their community or country. In fact, this is simply another way the Mahdi doctrine we mentioned above is fulfilled.

According to our research there are people who join these groups who reach such devastating states that upon receiving orders they kill without hesitation, like the addict dervishes of Hasan Sabah!

Whereas any sound person who carefully investigates such groups can easily detect many discrepancies and contradictions in their speech and incorrect, if not misleading information in their claims.

Whether scientific or spiritual, whatever question is posed to them, their answers are almost always nonsense and not worth taking into account.

When they're asked a question in regards to the future their answer is always ambiguous and shifty.

Their most popular method of deception is revealing some of the recent private matters of the newcomers, exposing them to the group.

When the state and the level of knowledge of those who join such groups are examined it is seen that every single one of them are seriously deprived of the knowledge of religion, especially concerning the spirit and the jinn, and they are resistive and antagonistic by nature. Because of this they become victims of beings whom they cannot even see.

Let me add that the jinn with whom some of these groups are in touch with have made an announcement immediately after this book was published, forbidding them from reading this book!

For clearly, those who read this book will doubtlessly see the truth behind the jinn.

In fact, if we examine the prayers performed by some of the people in these groups who claim to believe in Allah, their condition can be noticed straight away.

For example, some of them perform salat (!) three times a day, or once a day, in **standing** position, without bowing and prostrating, or only by prostrating!

They give alms (!) and in return they think all their sins have been forgiven by the "grand spirit" ruling them! While they continue to commit unlawful, sinful acts and crimes, they also continue to give charity so that their sins are cleansed!

In short, whichever religion the jinn ruling a particular group feels close to, or whichever belief system the majority of the group is affiliated with or inclined towards, that's the system used to govern the group.

Moreover, there are some who charge money to "cure the sick", making hundreds and millions off the public, even though none of the patients recover, other than maybe one or two per chance.

Thus, is how the good willed, pure, innocent people, who are in search of the truth and the reality, are fooled, deceived and led astray...

19

THE JINN AND WITCHCRAFT

At the root of necromancy, and all such nonsense, lies the "Science of Huddam" – commonly known as 'jinn dealing'…

Jinn dealing, an ancient concept especially in the region of Anatolia, is simply a technique of using the jinn as servants.

Some prayers have beings assigned to it who act as servants to that particular prayer assigned to it. They are known as the 'hadim' or the helpers of that prayer.

If someone sits down and repeats a certain prayer a specific number of times, a jinn appears in front of him. If the person makes a wish from the jinn without getting frightened of it, his wish will be granted immediately.

Or, if he wishes for the jinn to be his servant, the jinn immediately becomes his servant. There is a lot of formula related to this.

In the past there were books filled with such formulas, the most famous one being *"Kanzul Hawas"* (The Book of Hidden Sciences) …

However, it is important to note that there is a big difference between the science of Huddam and necromancy.

The difference is:

Necromancy is a game whereby the individuals who deal with it will always be toyed around by the jinn with whom they get in touch with. Like a rabbit fallen prey into the hands of a lion, the jinn will play with them as they like, and they can never be aware of this situation.

The science of Huddam, on the other hand, is a technique whereby the individual takes the jinn completely under his control and makes him do whatever he pleases, provided the formula is applied fully and correctly. He may even use the jinn to kill someone, for if the jinn who is possessed by the human does not obey the commands, he suffers greatly.

Therefore, this science offers absolute advantage humans, when compared to the other system.

Hence the science of Huddam, known only to a few, is much superior to necromancy. Because here the human takes the jinn under his control, whereas in the case of necromancy, directing the jinn or having them do something is not possible.

Here it is also necessary to understand the following point very clearly...

If an individual commences the application of a certain formula of the science of Huddam, but then he doesn't complete it out of fear or some other reason, this is the moment at which disaster will begin for him.

The jinn whom he was trying to take under his control will now have an advantageous position and take the individual under his control instead. Now the person is possessed and ruled by the jinn and there's nothing he can do about it. In the effort of gaining something better he loses what he already has.

For this reason, one should either not mess with the formulas of the science of Huddam at all, or if he starts it, he must complete the process till the very end no matter what.

As a matter of fact, the jinn will create disturbing noise and vision in order to prevent the formula from being fully applied. This can reach such scary extents that the person may feel like his house is being torn apart. Despite all of this he must keep his cool and persist on completing the formula...

As a matter of fact, the common misconception that one loses his mind when one engages in too much dhikr is based on this...

When one does dhikr without a guide and with knowledge of the formula, he inevitably generates a cipher, whereby the jinn that is connected to that cipher is automatically activated and able to possess the person. The person is neither aware of this situation, nor does he have the power to take the jinn under his control. He is now inescapably connected to the jinn…

This connection sometimes begins with hearing voices, either by ear or internally… Before this he may also smell different scents… Eventually he will begin to see the jinn in various forms and appearances.

Now if such a person shares his experiences with others he is immediately labelled 'crazy' or as 'having cracked it' and generally taken to hospital. However medical science is completely helpless in this field.

They will attempt to cure him using electro-shock, with no success!

Eventually the person will continue his life labelled as a 'psycho' or a 'harmless lunatic'…

If, however such a person is lucky enough to encounter someone who is an expert in this field, it may be possible for him to recover despite his condition.

Otherwise, they may never be cured from the state of delirium.

There is a profession that has been practiced for centuries, by even the most primitive tribes and communities…

This profession is called 'witchcraft' and its product is called 'black magic'…

The purpose of this profession is to take someone under control and make them do something against their will. Sometimes however, it is also practiced to cure the sick.

Black magic has been prohibited by all the Nabi and Rasuls who taught religions based on the reality of Allah…

All religions have prohibited the practice of black magic.

The religion of Islam also states black magic is impermissible and those who deal with it (directly or indirectly) have gone astray and left the boundaries of Islam.

The reason behind this prohibition is because one's will power is restricted or taken away by force, which means they are no longer responsible for their actions. This is unacceptable.

The practice of magic and witchcraft was most widespread during the time of Moses (pbuh). Precisely because magic was so widespread during that time, Moses (pbuh) fulfilled his duty by showing many miracles.

The essence and origin of witchcraft is based on the jinn…

Every single word in every verse contained in all of the sacred books and texts have 8 beings assigned to it as servants.

That is, 8 servants have been assigned as servants to every word comprising the origin of all of the sacred books revealed throughout the ages. Four of these are considered superior and are of the category of "angels" while the other four are considered inferior and are from the category of the jinn.

Repeating these words, a certain number of times based on the calculations of the **'Science of Abjad'** or reading these verses backwards would most certainly activate the jinn who are assigned as servants to these words and as a result, they will execute their effect on the people to whom they have been sent.

As a matter of fact, witchcraft consists of the effects that are produced by repeating a word or a sentence a specific number of times.

The most powerful counter effect to break the spell of witchcraft that I can recommend is the protection prayer I have mentioned previously…

This prayer can be recited by three or more people who come together in the house of the person who is under the spell of black magic and repeated 300 or 500 times…

If they can do this for three consecutive days, then it would be more effective. While the prayer is being recited, the person who has been influenced by black magic also needs to repeat this prayer.

Additionally, putting one's right hand on the head of the subject while repeating the prayer makes it much more effective...

Meanwhile, if a cup of water is placed in the middle and the prayers that are recited are blown into this cup then given to the subject to drink, it will be even more effective.

If an evil talisman is found either on the premises or on the subject, the most valid technique to neutralize this evil force is by placing it into acid, lemon juice or vinegar.

In order for the black magic to be more effective, magicians check the astrological hours, i.e. the 'hour of Venus' or the 'hour of Mars' etc. Detailed information concerning what these hours are can be found in our book "The Human Enigma."

Since witchcraft is not our main subject, I will only explain how it is achieved, without going into too much detail.

Today as science has revealed, the human brain radiates certain waves at every instant...

Let us share a passage from the daily newspaper *Hurriyet* to explain our argument better:

"THE HUMAN BODY WHICH WORKS AS AN ANTENNA RADIATES A CURRENT, WHICH COULD TRANSFER THOUGHTS OVER THOUSANDS OF KILOMETERS...

Los Angeles, (California) AP

Evidence that the human body may serve as the antenna and generate the power needed to transmit thoughts over thousands of miles was reported yesterday by Russian and American scientists.

Prof Dr. M. Kogan of the Popov Institute for the Study of radio Electronics and Communications in Moscow said the conclusions based on 1966 and 1967 experiments indicate thoughts may be conveyed by extremely long magnetic waves with crests ranging from twenty-five to one thousand miles apart.

Kogan said in a paper given at a symposium on extra-sensory perception sponsored by the University of California at Los Angeles that 'Telepathy via the electromagnetic field is possible in theory over any distance'.

Meanwhile, Dr. Thelma Moss, Assistant Professor of Medical Psychology at the University of California told the symposium that through their experiments, they have obtained findings very similar to Dr. Kogan's.

According to Kogan, the calculations indicate that the human body generates four to five times more the electrical current he thinks would be needed for long-distance telepathy."

As you can also see from this article the world of science has accepted the reality that the human brain continuously produces electromagnetic waves.

Detailed information concerning the kind of waves produced by the human brain and the activities of the brain made for this purpose can be found in our book *The Power of Prayer*.

So, whenever an individual repeats a certain word or a group of words continuously, the electromagnetic waves that he radiates are transformed into a kind of chipper. In this way, he establishes some kind of contact with a jinn whose structure is close to that of the chipper.

As a result of this contact, the electromagnetic waves whose structure is closest to that chipper affects that jinn. Whenever these waves are arranged correctly, they can force the jinn concerned to do whatever the individual wants him to do.

As they used to say in the past, if the individual goes on repeating this prayer and in spite of that, the jinn does not obey the order, then the jinn gets burned!'

Now, let us explain what this means:

When one repeatedly says a certain word or groups of words, the electromagnetic waves that are radiated through his brain will force a jinn who is compatible with that wavelength to do whatever the person wishes.

126

If the jinn does not comply, the electromagnetic power radiated by the person who repeats these words and prayers will eventually destroy the rays comprising the jinn, in other words, it will cause the jinn to burn.

This situation is very similar to a broadcast from a radio station transmitted at low frequency getting disturbed by the broadcast from another station transmitted at a more powerful frequency.

That is, the electromagnetic waves distributed by the high frequency radio station distort the waves of the low frequency radio station. In the same way, the electromagnetic waves produced by the individual engaged in such practices cause the jinn to die.

Therefore, the jinn are forced to obey the orders of these individuals who, with the waves they produce through witchcraft, can burn them.

I wonder if I have been able to explain...

20

THE EFFECT OF RECITING PRAYERS ON THE JINN

Generally, in Turkey and other Islamic countries, those who have been possessed by the jinn consult for a "reading" to treat their condition. That is, they seek someone with a strong breath to recite certain prayers on them to dispel the jinn.

In some regions there are 'hodjas' or 'sheiks' who are famous for dispelling the jinn.

Some are genuinely in pursuit of helping those who have fallen victim to the jinn; they neither request any monetary benefit nor do they accept gifts and favors in return.

On the other hand, many others with no real qualifications make a business out of it, exploiting vulnerable people who are desperately looking for relief...

To re-emphasize, those who are genuinely qualified will **never request or accept anything in return**, those who do are usually exploiters.

So, what actually happens during a reading that nullifies the effects of the jinn?

Let me try to explain this as best as I can:

I have already explained in the previous chapters that the make-up of the jinn is composed of certain rays and that humans are made of waves and the human body is constantly emitting various waves...

As I explained in the previous chapter on witchcraft the rays emitted by humans can be channeled to a specific point by consistently repeating a specific word, or a a group of words. For, there is no concept of time and space for these rays, they can reach any place at any time, based on how they are channeled.

Because of this when someone who is possessed by the jinn goes for a 'reading' the first thing that needs to be determined is the identity and state of the jinn who has possessed him.

After that, the jinn is ordered to release the individual, albeit whether he will accept this or not is doubtful.

After that, the person begins 'reading'. That is, he begins to recite certain words that spread waves which affect and damage the structural make-up of the jinn. It is as though he uses his brain a laser gun to shoot at the jinn!

At this point, the jinn has two choices. He can either comply with the orders and release the individual, or take the person who is reading under his control too…

Though there is also a third option for the jinn: to die! Some call this act 'burning the jinn.' That is, if the jinn does not release the individual, which is what generally happens, then he begins to burn until he eventually dies and the individual is saved.

Sometimes however, other jinn get involved, usually a family member, and this results in the burning of two or three jinn…

Many cases such as depression, frustration, feelings of suffocation, psychosis, seeing and hearing things, obsessive compulsive behaviors like constantly washing one's self etc. are almost always caused by the jinn.

Though because this has not yet been determined by medical science there is no medical treatment for such cases, other than using various tranquilizers to treat the 'symptoms' which only has a temporary effect.

In order to get satisfactory results, there is only one thing the world of medicine need to do and that is to accept the existence of the jinn and learn how to combat them using scientific methods.

Otherwise, it is impossible to achieve the desired results through electro-shock or tranquilizers. This will only drive people away from medical science in pursuit of "hodjas" and "sheikhs" who will simply take advantage of them.

21

THE DELUSION OF REINCARNATION

While explaining the non-Islamic methods the jinn use to possess people, we had briefly mentioned the concept of reincarnation. Let us now explore this subject in a little more depth:

Those who put forth the view of **reincarnation** claim the following:

Spirits have been created in pre-eternity then put into a physical body and sent down to earth to evolve…

However, not all spirits are equal in power, strength, comprehension, and the ability to evaluate. That is, they have been created unfairly, or they have come into existence on their own.

Hence a life of 50-60-70 years on Earth is not enough for its development… So, after death, Spirits (!) live in a certain place within the universe for a particular time… Then they come back to Earth with another body and personality to continue from where they had left off…

When it completes its life it dies again, and goes to the "waiting place" again… and then it comes back to Earth and continues its development!

This goes on until it completes its evolutionary process and reaches its highest capacity!

Once it becomes a perfect enlightened spirit it no longer comes back to Earth. However, this time it continues to evolve in other worlds…

And this goes on ad infinitum…

For thousands of years, many people, particularly those in India and the surrounding regions, have believed in reincarnation (*tanasukh*).

Tanasukh is commonly accepted by people whose level of knowledge is limited and below average due to their brain structure and primitive thinking. What I mean by this is their capacity in this particular field is below the average. Being insufficient in one field does not mean one is insufficient in all fields. Those who have read about the structure of the brain in the section on the body, in the chapter on humans, will surely understand what I mean.

It is easy to discern that ninety nine percent of all those who believe in reincarnation are in contact with the spirits (!) or more openly, with the jinn, and they get this idea from them.

As I have previously mentioned, the jinn initially present themselves as the spirit of so and so and they display certain extraordinary activities to fool people and take under their control.

However, in the following stages things start to change and their real motive becomes obvious.

The real reason behind why the jinn make contact with humans is to lead them astray, diverting them towards wrong beliefs and making them lose their faith.

Because of this, they lead people into wrong beliefs, particularly on two main topics:

Spiritualism is the name given to all systems of belief that accept the existence of dimensions beyond the material realm, while Spiritism is the name given to a school of thought whose members deal with calling and communicating with the spirits(!).

So, after the initial stage is over, those who are in contact with the jinn, or the "spirits" fall into two incorrect beliefs:

1. Reincarnation, in other words tanasukh.

2. Accepting the pantheist point of view as 'Uluhiyyah'

I shall try to explain the first one in this section.

First of all, let us examine the quotations extracted from the Quran by those who promote the idea of **'Reincarnation'** among the Muslim communities:

These who defend the idea of being **'reborn'** into another body have been fooled by the jinn and in order to prove their arguments more effectively, they use the verses below:

> **How can you deny that the Names of Allah comprise your essence (in accord with the meaning of the letter B when you were lifeless (unaware of your essential reality) and He brought you to life again He will cause you to die (from the state of thinking you are only the body), and again He will bring you to life (purify you from confining your existence to your body and enable you to live in a state of consciousness) ... eventually you will see your reality.[39]**

Explanation:

O mankind, how can you try to cover the reality of **"ALLAH"** when you were **DEAD**, unconscious of your essence and unable to control your body, and **HE BROUGHT YOU TO LIFE; with the knowledge He disclosed to you and allowed you to administer your body... HE WILL MAKE YOU DIE AGAIN** that is, cut your ties to your body and separate your consciousness from your biological body, **THEN AGAIN HE WILL BRING YOU TO LIFE**, when your biological body becomes useless your consciousness will transform into a wave body and move on to another level of life until Doomsday, **AND EVENTUALLY YOU WILL SEE YOUR REALITY**; there is no coming back, you will ascend to higher dimensions and unite with Allah in your essence.

As can be seen, the verse above does not in any way imply countless returns to Earth or returning to the world again and again until one is

---

[39] Quran 2:28

purified and enlightened. If that were really the case, then this would have been stated in this verse or other verses in the Quran.

> **"You turn the night into day and turn the day into night. You bring the living out of the dead and the dead out of the living. You give provision (life sustenance) to whom You will without account."[40]**

Explanation:

YOU TURN THE NIGHT INTO DAY AND TURN THE DAY INTO NIGHT means, nothing is left in a particular state, everything is substituted with its opposite.

YOU BRING THE LIVING OUT OF THE DEAD, you place those who are not limited by matter under the constraints of the physical world and body **AND THE DEAD OUT OF THE LIVING**, you make those DIE who appear to be alive in their bodies made of flesh and bones, i.e. you release them from the limitations of matter. You give countless sustenance to those you wish.

As can be seen from this verse too, there is no direct or indirect implication about coming back to Earth again and again for the purpose of evolution!

However, it is most unfortunate that people who have been fooled by the jinn change the meanings of these verses according to their way of thinking in attempt to prove their claims.

In fact, when you get to know these people a little closer in almost every case it is seen that they do not possess the slightest knowledge on neither Islam nor the Quran.

---

[40] Quran 3:27

And Allah causes you to grow from the earth gradually like a plant (the body that comes from the earth continues its life as consciousness).

"Then He will return you into it and again extract you from it."

"And Allah has made for you the earth an exhibition (living environment)."

"So that you may traverse therein, on spacious ways."[41]

Explanation:

ALLAH CAUSED YOU TO GROW FROM THE EARTH LIKE A PLANT, means Allah created Adam, your ancestor and the first human on earth from the element 'earth', that is, Allah created the human body from a compound consisting of minerals and water.

THEN HE WILL RETURN YOU INTO IT; means Allah will cut your ties to your body and free you from the limitation of matter allowing the physical body to decompose back into the earth … Meanwhile will continue your life as a conscious being in the Intermediary Realm (barzakh).

THEN ALLAH WILL AGAIN EXTRACT YOU FROM IT: That is, when the day of reconning (the day when people will have to face with the final results of what they've done) comes, ALLAH will raise you again. However, this time, Allah will raise you in a different manner, not like the gradual growth of your physical body on earth but in the state that you were put into the grave, and from this He will form a NEW body for you, suitable to that particular environment.

ALLAH HAS MADE FOR YOU THE EARTH AN EXHIBITION: ALLAH created the planet Earth in a way that will enable you to live on it with your physical body.

SO THAT YOU MAY TRAVERSE THEREIN, ON SPACIOUS WAYS meaning that you may go around and travel wherever you like in the world and live at any place you wish.

---

[41] Quran 71:17-20

Let's examine the deeper meaning of two words in this verse:

In Sufism the word earth refers to the intellect. When the above two verses are read in this respect, the meaning becomes, "Allah has made for you the intellect an exhibition, that is a vast area, so that you may traverse therein, through the many neural networks and ways of thoughts…

That is to say, human beings have been given a structure enabling them to travel between various thoughts and in addition to that; they have been given the Quran, which shows them the *Sirat al-Mustaqim* (The Correct Path) upon which Allah wants them to walk.

I don't know if I have been able to demonstrate the vein primitiveness of those who are possessed by the jinn trying to prove the validity of reincarnation by using religion.

I think I have put forward enough information to show the insufficiency of those who lack knowledge of Islam and the Quran…

Yet they continue to make claims like "The Quran does not contain a single verse rejecting the idea of reincarnation" while building their ideas on false foundations.

I can disprove their claims simply by sharing one verse even though there are several more verses on this subject.

Here is the translation of one of the verses in the Quran rejecting the idea of reincarnation, namely *tanasukh*.

1. **And say, "My Rabb (the protective Names within my essence), I seek refuge in You from the incitements of the satans (that call to corporeality)."**

2. **"And I seek refuge in You (your protective Names within my essence), my Rabb, lest they be around me."**

3. **When death comes to one of them, he says, "My Rabb, send me back (to the worldly life)."**

4. **"So that I might do righteousness in that which I left behind (i.e. a faithful life that I did not heed or give importance to; the potential that I did not utilize and activate)." NO! (It is**

impossible to go back!) His words are invalid! (His request is unrecognized in the system) and behind them is a barrier (an isthmus; a difference of dimension) until the Day they are resurrected (they cannot go back; reincarnation, being re-born for another worldly life, is not possible!).[42]

Now let us examine the meaning of these verses:

In order to teach the Muslims how to protect themselves from the jinn with satanic qualities, Allah tells them to say the following:

"My Rabb, I seek refuge in You from the incitements, false assumptions and conjectures of the evils and the jinn with satanic attributes, that will lead me away from faith…"

AND I TAKE REFUGE IN YOU O MY RABB FROM THEM BEING AROUND ME, in my presence and vicinity, and their attempts to make contact with me…

For they will suggest wrong ideas to me and I will mistakenly think I may come back to this world…

And if I die with this belief, I will say MY RABB, SEND ME BACK TO THE WORLD SO THAT I MAY I PERFORM RIGHT DEEDS TO COMPENSATE FOR THE LIFE THAT I HAVE LOST and die as one who knows the reality…

BUT NO, THESE WORDS regarding reincarnation ARE INVALID AND MEANINGLESS, they have no validity in the system of Allah.

BEHIND THEM IS A BARRIER (Barzakh) preventing them from rising until the day of resurrection when ALL of the humans will be resurrected… That is, their connection to their physical bodies has been cut off, their ties to the Earth has ended, they have moved on to another dimension… This is referred to as the Realm of the Grave in Islamic literature.

---

[42] Quran 23:97-100

So, this is the interpretation of one of the verses, demonstrating the invalidity of reincarnation.

Now, let us come have a look at another method they employ to prove reincarnation.

However, allow me to state once again that the main reason why these subjects could not be explained more openly in the past is because those who were influenced by the jinn were scared of being ridiculed and hence refrained from talking about their situation.

On the other hand, you will see that as we refute their alleged evidences, when the existence of the jinn is declared and accepted, the inside story behind the mystery of these complex events will become very clear.

If after all of this, one still insists on making such claims, then this can simply be regarded as a clear indication that they do not want to take back what they have said.

Apart from religious methods, other evidences that are put forth by those who believe in reincarnation are in the following areas:

a. Dreams...

b. Déjà vu experiences...

c. Amnesia (Loss of memory)

d. Direct remembrance of past lives.

Let us now explore each of these to show how they cannot prove the validity of reincarnation.

22

DREAMS – DÉJÀ VU – ECMNESIA – PAST LIVES

During sleep, one is free from the limitations of his body, in proportion with the sensitivity of his brain, and thus begins to ascend… This ascension may either be vertical or horizontal.

If the ascension takes place horizontally, he may travel around the world and see places he has never seen before, depending on how much he can release himself from the conditioning of his bodily senses, as many factors play a role in this…

It is at this level that he may encounter the jinn…

I would like to give an example from my own life. In 1965, while I was going to Hajj (Pilgrimage to Mecca) by using the motorway, I went to the South East region of Turkey and I stopped by the city of Gaziantep. While I was there, I went to see the Colonel N. who was a judge in the army and was one of my close friend's uncle in law. When I went there and saw the premises of the military barracks and its garden, I was very much surprised, because I knew that I had definitely seen that place before.

Now, those who believe in reincarnation will immediately make the following interpretation: 'It is most certain that in your previous life, you were either an army officer or a soldier and you must have done your military service there, which is why you can remember that place'.

In fact, what has been sighted does not have any connection with what they claim. Because, even though I cannot state an exact date when, I remember very clearly seeing the exact scene in a dream some time before. If it were possible for me to have lived in that place before, then surely some changes should have taken place since that time.

As I said, the situation is very simple and clear to understand. During sleep, the upper part of the body, also referred to as **'the human'** or the **'astral body'** leaves the physical body and enters the astral plane, making a horizontal tour. Clearly, I had seen this place during one of these tours.

Apart from this, many of my dreams whether related to the past or the future have actualized in exactly the same manner as I have shared above.

So, to wrap it up, all such dreams (referred to as **'ru'yah' in Arabic**, which means **'sight'**) takes place during the sleep as a result of the horizontal ascension of the upper structure of the body.

As for vertical ascensions...

Let us start with an example...

As I have previously explained from the scientific view point, the concept of time and place is relative, it is experienced differently by everyone...

For example, imagine that you are in an infinitely big desert, and you are walking in the middle of a long caravan. It is so long that you can't see its beginning or end. The places that you can see and recognize are limited to a distance of only a few meters within the scope of your eye sight.

Now, the places that you see within a certain period of time, say within one hour, will be considered **'past'** after that hour is over and you've walked all that distance. The area that you're walking through at that particular instant would then become the **'present'** for you while only an hour ago it was the **'future'**...

Similarly, for someone walking behind you, your current position would be regarded as the **'future'** for them and their current position at that moment, i.e their "present" would be the **'past'** for you.

Now consider a helicopter entering the scene, picking you up and rising towards the sky vertically. What will happen then?

While the area you had just seen within a few hundred meters were regarded as your 'present', the places you are seeing now as you rise higher and higher will begin to expand and what you had seen an hour ago and what had become the 'past' for you, will now become the 'present' and hence the past and future will slowly diminish while the 'present' continues to expand.

Eventually you may reach a point at which you may be able to see the entire caravan and desert… While time and space is still applicable to those in the caravan, you will have become freed of these concepts. Your ascension will have saved you from this limitation.

So, we may conclude that to the extent that one is able to ascend vertically (we do not yet have sufficient knowledge on what causes vertical ascension in dreams) and free himself from his physical conditioning, he will begin to encompass the past and the future…

For nothing that is nonexistent becomes existent and nothing that exists becomes nonexistent. Based on this principle, everything that has transpired in the "past" (the relative past, based on your current position) is present and existent as certain wavelengths in space.

If we had a powerful radio in our hands that is capable of interpreting these waves into signals that our ears can analyze and hear or if we had a television set that could show these waves to our eyes, we would then be able to see the past as if we were living it now.

Likewise, the future descends from the *heavens*, which in Islamic terminology means "dimensions" referring to levels of different heights, in the form of waves at every instant.

In other words, depending on the extent of the vertical ascension one is able to make, one may observe the 'past' and the 'future' in his 'present' moment.

This is why some people make vertical ascensions in their dreams and go to those times, experiencing those events almost as if they are living it. When they come back to earth, that is when they wake up in the dimension of the physical body, they are able to recount their experiences.

Anyone who believes in reincarnation and observes this event would immediately attribute it to the previous life of that person, interpreting it as the individual remembering his previous life. However, it is most certain that it has no connection whatsoever with something that has been lived in a past life.

Déjà vu is similar to this.

The individual sees places and events that he had never seen before through dreams, but then forgets them completely.

Besides dreams, it is also possible to see visions generated by the jinn.

As for ecmnesia, the person is put to sleep through hypnosis and sent to a period 5-10 or 40-50 years in the past, then asked to explain the life at that time…

However, if the hypnotized person is sent to a time period below his current age, for example to 100-200 years before he was born, then he starts to explain the life of another person who lived in another place as if it were his own life…

So, what is the reality behind this? It is actually quite simple…

I had already explained that during necromancy sessions one thinks he is making contact with the 'spirits' while in fact he is making contact with the jinn who are compatible with his make-up. I had also mentioned that the life span of a jinn is 10-15 times more than that of a human. In fact, there are those who were born 1350 years ago are still alive today.

Moreover, many things that are 'unknown' to us are not unknown to the jinn; they are visible to them.

Now the moment a person falls asleep, the circuits of his brain related to the faculties of thought and reasoning become ineffective. Therefore, the brain becomes prone to all kinds of stimuli and influences.

While in this state, the body, together with all its functions goes under the influence of a jinn whose frequency is most compatible with that person's make-up. **From that moment onwards, it is no longer the person who we are in contact with, but the jinn who has taken over.**

After this point, you can take the individual to the past or the future as much as you will, he will be able to answer all your questions, because for the jinn, this knowledge is no secret.

If you say, "But if we go to a period before the birth of that individual, then we encounter some other personality, who is clearly the individual's spirit who lived before in the body of another person! So, this is the proof that the spirit of the same human being lives in other bodies with different personalities" …

Then I will give the following answer:

In such a circumstance, rather than that individual, it is the jinn who starts giving examples from the life of another person who happened to live somewhere else.

Meanwhile, all emotional reactions the hypnotized person's body gives as he supposedly remembers these are generated in his brain by the **manipulation of the jinn.**

It is common knowledge today that computers can stimulate sensory areas of the brain with electrical signals directed to specific regions of the brain connected with certain emotions. These pulses when given appropriately stimulate an electrochemical response from the targeted cells, which ripples across the brain, making the individual cry or laugh. The world of medical science is well aware of this situation.

Hence the jinn send impulses to the brain of the hypnotized person to create the behavioral reactions that are needed.

Those who witness this cannot really understand what is going on; they simply assume that these reactions are due to the person's experiences in the past.

A few years ago, a jinn appeared as angel to a group of people in Ankara, claiming his name to be **'Basheer-al Kiraam'.** He explained in detail all the stages of the battle that took place between *Sultan Alparslan* and *Romanos Diogenes* in 1071. This was a truly amazing event. The "angel" told them how the war was carried out and narrated the conversations that took place between Alparslan and Diogenes from their own mouths, in their own original words and accents, after which he translated them. The people who witnessed this event were fascinated to such degree that some of them even devoted themselves to this "angel" as though he were a god.

Thus, in such events, it is always a jinn that appears through the person who is hypnotized; it is a jinn that talks to and answers the questions of the people there …

Therefore, there is no such thing as reincarnation, the truth behind it is as I have described.

Finally, let us move on to the fourth point, people remembering their 'past lives'…

This also clearly has to do with relationship with the jinn…

Many elderly people especially those from the region of Anatolia are closely familiar with these events that are now being modernized and presented as reincarnation…

When I previously talked about 'humans who are unaware of their subservience to the jinn' I had touched on the topic of reincarnation and noted that I will cover more on it in proceeding chapters…

So let me now explain:

In the case of ecmnesia the same story about one's past life is being repeated. However, this time, he's recalling it not during his sleep but in his awake state.

So, what is making this individual talk about his past life?

It is very simple…

A jinn begins to manipulate the brain of the person without him being aware and talks from his mouth, giving information about the life of another person who had lived in the past, as though it was the life of the person through whose mouth he is talking. That is, the person is more like a robot, used and controlled by the jinn…

Since others who are witnessing this are not able to see what is really going on due to their sensory limitations, they are unable to reach the truth behind it, and hence claim it is due to reincarnation.

To conclude, all examples that are put forth to 'prove reincarnation' are rendered invalid once the existence of the jinn – whose make up I have already explained – is accepted and known. In this light, the truth behind all such events becomes apparent and clear.

For this reason, I would like to underline that spiritualism, parapsychology or other such concepts are indeed all different versions of the same phenomenon related to the jinn, who were well known and accepted in the past, but are being denied today simply because their reality isn't understood.

Whether in the name of spiritism or through other means, it is not possible to benefit from the jinn. They will most certainly speak correctly up to a certain point, but will eventually cause divergence, leading people astray and causing harm to those who believe in them… However, due to the nature of humans, they will almost never know this.

As I have already pointed out before, whenever you examine those who believe in the jinn, it is evident that they have one thing in common.

Every one of them is curious, good willed and likes to do research. But they have no knowledge whatsoever on religion, especially on Islam. Most importantly, they deny the reality of the jinn which has an important place in the 'Quran' and are thus easy targets for the jinn who fool them in the guise of 'spirits'…

Today, in Turkey there are many associations who deal with spiritism or necromancy, and invisible beings who make contact through these associations. However, they always seem to work secretly behind the scenes… Nowadays for example they think they're receiving directions from the aliens…

They never accept into their circle those who do not believe in them… If by accident such a person ends up joining them, they never let him ask any questions or argue with them in any way.

For they if they do, the jinn with whom these associations are in contact with know that their lies will become obvious. For this reason, they try to protect their status by trying not to get degraded in any way in the eyes of those who believe in them.

23

ALIENS!!?

One of the most popular topics of recent years, not only among the public but also among the intellectuals, is no doubt "Flying Saucers" …

Many people around the world, most of whom are from the US and some countries in Europe claim to have sighted these flying saucers, which supposedly carry alien beings from other worlds and dimensions who apparently visit Earth to make contact with humans…

There are many different views on "Unidentified Flying Objects" or in short UFO's…

News on this subject can be found in even the most prestigious magazines and newspapers published in America and Europe giving significant coverage to those who have made contact and their experiences.

Even if we accept that 95% of the news and information on this subject is fraud, that is, even if we assume that these things that are seen by these individuals are actually nothing other than the shooting stars, clusters of clouds, air balloons or other such similar scenes, there is still a 5% chance that there is some reality to these claims, especially considering the state of the individuals who have seen these objects and the ways in which these objects appeared to them.

The very fact that there is a 'UFO' department in the US Ministry of Defense and archives of photos of these objects is sufficient to suggest that this is somewhat serious.

Recently, an interview was published in the daily newspaper *Cumhuriyet*, regarding a teacher who claimed to have seen a flying saucer while he was in the classroom with his students. According to the teacher, there were beings coming out from this saucer which nobody else in the classroom was able to see. Here is an excerpt from this interview, reported by Mr. Turhan ILGAZ:

"Approximately two years ago, a teacher was conducting an exam in the Pangaltı Armenian High School. After she had handed out the questions to her students, she sat at her desk and all of a sudden, a scene appeared on the walls of the classroom.

She said that 'It was just like a movie. There, in front of me was a flying saucer. And then a man, who looked just like us came out from it'."

The woman who saw this is a psychic and she communicated with the newcomer telepathically. After this initial meeting, they met many times again.

So, this is one way of encountering flying saucers...

So, what is the truth behind this?

Do flying saucers actually exist?

Are there other human species living on other planets?

Are the beings wanting to make contact with humans also humans who live on other planets or are they other types of beings?

This is surely one of the most interesting topics of recent times!

And the biggest mistake that is made in this area is "asking the scientists"!

The subject of aliens should never be asked to the scientists!

There isn't a single scientist, neither in Turkey nor in the world who can answer the questions relating to aliens. Whoever seeks advice from the scientists on this matter will surely be mistaken!

WHY?

Let us know first of all that **'science'** is formed within a particular system, which relies on using observable objects and data that already exists. The people who examine this data in detail and conduct extensive research on them reach a conclusion and establish a system, which finally produces that particular branch of science.

It is the people who create that branch of science who are referenced as the scientists who are specialized in that particular field.

Let me explain this by an example.

The human body exists; there are people who examine it and conduct researches on it to decipher how it works and hence they have produced a branch of science. Thus, there is an observable data and system here. This means there is a scientist whose field of expertise is the human body, i.e. the doctors, medical professors, neurologists, etc.

Do we have all the data concerning the aliens? Has there been systematic research carried out with the data that we have? Has anyone followed a systematic line of investigation on these matters to determine how they really function?

Of course, the answer to all of these is NO.

This being the case, we may conclude that there is no branch of science based on the aliens nor are there any scientists!

You may, if you wish, ask this to a doctor or a professor of law. You can also ask an ASTRONOMY professor!

Needless to say, they are all equal individuals who have the same level of knowledge on this particular subject despite the fact that they have all become professors in their own branches!

One of them is a professor on the subject of law; the other one is a professor on the human body and the other one is a professor studying the stars.

However, there isn't a single professor on the subject of the **ALIENS!**

This is not only the issue in Turkey but the whole world!

After making this emphasis, let us all pay attention to the following point.

In recent years, various incidents have occurred relating to this subject. One of these is the publication made by the Russian TASS news agency, claiming that children playing at a park in a city in Russia made contact with beings from outer space!

The other incident is the crop circles that have appeared in the grain fields of southern England.

The following article has been extracted from the Magazine of Science and Technology that is partly attached to the newspaper *Cumhuriyet* dated 5th of October 1991.

THE DEFENDERS OF THE UFO'S HAVE BEEN CAUGHT

In England, those who have made the heavenly drawings and the lines in the wheat fields have been exposed. Here is the inside story of this event the UFO defenders loved, but which made scientists work really hard!

'This is without doubt the most wonderful moment of my research' marveled Pat Delgado, the famous researcher on UFO's who was saying the following after he had seen the wheat field in Sevenoaks, England: 'No human could have done this'.

Delgado was saying these by gazing at the wheat plants that were created in such a perfect way. The plants had been laid clockwise on the ground in the shape of an almost perfect circle. There were other shapes that were seen as the elongations of this circle: Antennas, a semi-circle and a line which was in the form of a strip. The circles that were seen in Sevenoaks were the last of the hundreds of similar shapes that had been seen in Southern England since the last three years. For Delgado, who has been researching and writing on this subject, these circles were the perfect proof showing the existence of a higher level of intelligence.

However, the joy of Delgado did not last long. Graham Brough, a reporter from the Today newspaper had watched two landscape painters making up these drawings. David Chorley, aged 62 and Douglas Bower aged 67 had created the Sevenoaks circle while Brough was with them all through the process. Moreover, the duo revealed that for the past 13 years, they have been sneaking around southern England, fashioning as many as 25 to 30 new circles each growing season.

The explanations of these two people had clarified the mystery with which the whole of England and the world had been interested. Many interesting ideas had been put forth about how these circles on the ground were formed. The flying saucers, the electromagnetic field and the microwaves in the atmosphere were only a few of them.

Actually, the method used by these two hoaxers did not have any relation with extraordinary powers. They were using a wooden plank with a length of 1.2 meters and a ball of string. Bower was standing at the center of the field that they've chosen and holding the plank in an upright position. The rope was tied to the wooden stick at the height of a knee. When Chorley turned around, Bower and holding the rope very tight, then the wheat plants were going down sideways.

Chorley and Bower had created their first drawing in the field in 1978. By making the wheat plants lean sideways, their aim was to give the impression that the UFO's had landed on that field. However, for three years long their works could not catch the attention of anyone. These shapes were spotted in the press for the first time in 1981. The reason why these two men had confessed what they've done was due to the fact that the researchers on this subject had asked the government to give them some financial support.

So, are we going to categorize those who have seen these sightings as people with **'Psychological Disorders'** or as people whose psychology is **'extremely sensitive'?**

Certainly not!

Well, if that is the case then attributing this topic to the planet Venus, which is observed only for about two hours at sunset, will indeed be a baseless claim.

What is most definite is that by whatever name they may be called, there are certain number of beings either living among us, or in the atmosphere or inside our solar system and they transmit certain images to us from time to time.

However, our biggest mistake regarding this subject comes from our habit of only accepting the existence of the things that are validated by our five senses and disregarding everything else.

Throughout the centuries we have been shown time and time again that many things do exist outside the scope of our five senses. As technology developed, we became forced to accept the existence of many things that we believed were **'non-existent'** in the past. Yet instead of taking a lesson from all of this, we still mistakenly deny the existence of the things that exceed the limits of our five senses and our current technology. Indeed, this is a big shame.

So, what are these extraterrestrial beings we call the '**ALIENS**'?

Since there has been no case where an alien has actually been caught by humans so that the necessary examinations can be carried out, nobody has valid evidence to make any claims about the aliens. For this reason, there can be no expert in this field either.

However, we can't just simply assume that the aliens were absolutely nonexistent fifty years ago and then all of a sudden, they miraculously appeared either!

On the other hand, we know there were various beings co-inhabiting this world for centuries and centuries alongside the humans. While some called them '**ghosts**,' others called them '**spirits**' or '**fairies**' and some called them the '**jinn**' or the '**giants**'.

These beings who display specific characteristics and who sometimes appear to be helping humans while at other times challenge the human willpower, were also called the "jinn" during the period when the Quran was revealed.

Regardless of the degree of your cultural and educational level or the conditioning with which you have blocked yourself there is an undeniable truth. There are beings who are not always perceivable that exist in this world other than humans, and the majority of the people acknowledge and accept them, albeit under different names.

Neither denial will make them disappear nor acceptance will bring any benefits! In fact, denial only gives them a wider space of entertainment. For we know that whatever we may call them, these beings take great pleasure from deceiving and ruling humans and making them pursue hopeless futile dreams.

Surely, we couldn't have expected these beings who are free from the limitations of a physical body to behave differently towards the humans who are extremely limited with their physical body! While there are multitudes of people within their reach whom they can deceive and have fun with, surely it is impossible to think they will not take advantage of this opportunity!

The Quran points to this reality with the following verse:

"O community of jinn, you have truly possessed (misled from reality) **the vast majority of mankind."** [43]

So, whatever name you like to give them whether it be the **'ALIENS'** or the **'JINN'** - the name usually used in religious terminology and by the elderly people- one of the greatest quality of these beings is to take the humans under their domination and then drag them into beliefs and behaviors that conflict with the reality.

These invisible beings we call the jinn approach each society with the conditioning and the cultural values of that particular population to take them under their ruling. Similarly, they approach individuals with ideas and visuals related to whatever the tendency and motivation of that person is.

In general, they dominate the great majority without them being aware.

The people they rule are usually people who claim to accept the religion of Islam, or those who do not accept it at all.

Their way of deceiving those who do not accept the Islamic belief is by imposing the concept of reincarnation…

Indeed, their biggest entertainment in recent years has been the act of introducing themselves to the mankind as extraterrestrial beings from outer space and other galaxies.

In actual fact, these beings live on the earth and they occupy the planet earth's atmosphere. Because they are very clever beings and have the capacity to move and act very fast, they can deceive and fool the people very easily.

Their way of deceiving the people is almost always by sending impulses to their brains. Based on the frequencies of these impulses the individuals think they are hearing or seeing certain things.

Whereas they're not actually seeing or hearing anything at all! And since nobody else can perceive what this person is perceiving they simply deny his state. To give an example, it is like the state of one who is dreaming while they are actually awake.

---

[43] Quran 6:128

Their most popular method of deceiving those with beliefs other than Islam, is through necromancy and alien contact.

Generally, these are naive people whose cultural upbringing and knowledge is insufficient and hence they assume that they are actually making contact with aliens from outer space or with the spirits of their loves ones who have passed away. I will explain this point in more detail and give you all the evidence in the related section ahead.

It's simple to determine and expose the lies of the jinn who introduce themselves as beings from outer space:

Ask them to give you a solid tangible instrument or a device that is touchable! They will never be able to do this!

Because, the jinn can't go further than **manipulating one's faculty of imagination!**

They constantly target individuals whose brains are very sensitive and they manipulate their visual center by generating various images. And when required, they trigger the sections in the brain related to fear and illusion to make them see the things, which in reality do not exist at all. Hence by giving them fear, they can easily control and possess them!

These beings who introduce themselves as the **aliens** are in fact the **jinn** and their bodies are made of radial waves. They constantly make promises and give false hopes about the future, imposing the idea that they are the real **'MAHDI'**, the **'MESSIAH'** or the long-awaited leader for humanity. They pledge the coming of the **'GOLDEN AGE'** and sometimes even give specific dates. As soon as that date arrives and their prophecies aren't fulfilled, they cover up their lies and create new false hopes with statements like **'Well, the necessary conditions have not been formed, you couldn't perform your duties in the manner that was required of you, therefore it has been postponed to a later date'.**

Getting fooled by these beings who create nothing other than illusions similar to 'a flying saucer, a balloon or some humanlike image' and then introducing themselves as 'extraterrestrial beings from outer space' is simply the result of insufficient knowledge.

The **ALIENS(!)** who only give misinformation and deception and misguide humanity have so many methods to deceive humans it's really difficult to list all of them here.

Therefore, in whatever form or shape they appear to you, whether it be 'ALIENS' or as 'Gnostics or Saints' that have lived in the past, please be absolutely sure that they are without a doubt the JINN and they carry Satanist qualities of which humans have been explicitly warned in the past!

They constantly provoke people into imagining things that are not real, triggering fear and anxiety to use them like puppets in their hands.

If we want to protect ourselves from these beings, the first thing we should do is to expose their lies so that their real intentions can become evident... When they realize that they cannot fool you within a certain period of time, they will eventually disclose themselves.

In such scenarios, it is of paramount importance to recite the prayer I have previously shared, which will create a protective magnetic shield around you. In my experience this prayer is extremely effective in exposing the jinn.

Even though I'm fully aware that those who do not believe me will make fun of what I'm going to say, I'm still going to state with certainty that all of these flying saucers and those who give us the impression that they have arrived here by the aid of the flying saucers are nothing other than the JINN!

In the past, the jinn were visible to the humans. They were seen in forms that resembled humans or animals, and the locations where they were sighted included places like the village roads and the graveyards as well as the haunted houses of Anatolia or the west. Today, they deceive those who do not believe in and give value to the past by appearing as flying saucers...

It is almost as though by deceiving the people with these new methods the jinn are making fun of and taking revenge from those who mock them and do not believe in them.

In actual fact, there is no difference between the visions of the flying saucers and the visions seen by those who suddenly encounter strange figures while walking through the dark village roads in the middle of the night. They're different visuals but same in the sense that humans aren't able to fully perceive them though they have accepted them to be normal.

A materialist medical expert may perhaps interpret this as hallucination... But for someone who believes in metaphysics and the dimensions beyond matter, they are both the same.

155

These beings to which the Quran refers to as the jinn, but who are known by other names in other places, do not possess a physical structure yet they can appear as a human, an animal, or any material shape they desire, mostly in desolate places. It does not matter where and how they are seen, on the village roads or the walls, or as a human coming out of a flying saucer, they are all the same.

As I have already explained, whenever and wherever they wish, the jinn are able to make their immaterial bodies appear as material...

This is very much like the case of electromagnetic waves that we see every day on the TV screen whereby the waves that are transmitted to the screen can be seen in the air before they actually are transformed onto the screen. Just imagine watching TV but not on the TV screen, but in empty space. In other words, rather than watching on the TV screen the images that some electromagnetic waves have produced, you are watching them in the air.

Here, I'm reminded of a hadith I recently read by the Rasul of Allah (saw). From what I remember, the meaning of it was as follows.

"As the world approaches its final period, the jinn will start to become visible on the planet earth and they will try to make contact with the humans in various ways.'

This topic made me remember this hadith. You may either wish to make a connection between the hadith and these events, or not, it is entirely up to you!

According to the information in religious sources, the teachings of the Sufi masters and the outcome of my thought process and contemplation, the beings referred to as 'humans' live only on the planet Earth

And the jinn are the only **'conscious'** beings whose life bears a great resemblance to humans.

Besides these, there are no other beings that exist on other planets that resemble humans or the jinn with a physical-material body. It is for this reason that no matter how much mankind makes progress and relies on science, they will never be able to find any being that has a physical body like themselves in any other planet. All beings that resemble humans or appear in other forms are the jinn.

There is life on other planets too. However, the life and vitality on other planets are beyond the scope of our five senses, in fact some are at microscopic levels. This type of life exists even on the Sun.

On the other hand, there are many allegations that physical pieces of metal and various kinds of other tangible matter pertaining to the flying saucers have been found. Since these pieces are extremely small in size, we may infer that the jinn who are comprised of rays use their electrical power to transform these tiny metals into other forms, similar to how coal turns into diamond under high pressure.

Our final and definite word on this subject is that the images of the flying saucers and all other things similar to these sightings belong to the jinn, much similar to illusions created by a medium.

24

WHO ARE THE PSYCHICS REALLY MAKING CONTACT WITH?

Let's assume that apart from the human species, there is at least one other kind of life form – regardless of what we call it - with whom we are living together and with whom we are in contact.

These beings send impulses composed of specific waves and frequencies to mediums, whose brains are sensitive enough to receive them, in order to create certain ideas in their minds.

So, what shall we call them?

You can call them the SPIRITS...

Or the JINN

Or the ALIENS...

Or, if you wish, you may call them by another name, or they may call themselves by another name.

The fact is there are invisible beings who introduce themselves to us in various forms and with various names.

The Quran has introduced these beings to us with the name 'JINN' not to mention the extensive warnings made by Muhammad (saw).

In the past the jinn, who always hide their true identity, introduced themselves as spirits, in particular the spirits of saints who lived in the past.

These beings who communicate with the people by using nick names such as 'Mawlana Jalaladdin al-Rumi', 'Yunus Emre' and 'Abdulqadir al-Jilani', begun to carry out their mission by presenting the truth of Sufism and recommending ALLAH to all the people who don't know anything about ISLAM or SUFISM as if they are fully aware of this subject.

However, because their real objective is to divert people away from their beliefs, in time they started to impose the idea that all the religions including Islam are no longer valid.

Their next step following this was their claim to be ALIEN BEINGS from outer space who actually rule the entire world behind the scenes.

During the years 1935 to 1940, these beings were claiming that they were the spirits. However, as from the beginning of the 1960's, they started to claim they are EXTRATERRESTIALS.

Following their first declaration in 1962, the association that apparently received these declarations published a book named 'THE PLAN OF THE LOYAL ONES / THE MISSION OF THE GOLDEN AGE' in which they introduced themselves as THE SPIRITUAL PLAN, THE ORGANIZER. In time they changed this to the EXTRATERRESTRIALS. Despite the fact that at the onset, they attempted to make extensive explanations on certain serious topics, over time they literally started mocking and making fun of people, turning this into a form of entertainment for themselves.

25

WHY DO THE JINN HIDE THEIR REAL IDENTITY?

The jinn, who have introduced themselves as the spirits and extraterrestrials between the 1930s until mid 1986, have for the first time openly declared that they are in fact the beings referenced in the Quran as the **'Jinn'.**

In their own words, they disclose their real identity and the reasons why they concealed this in the following way:

The World Brotherhood Union, the GOLDEN AGE BOOK OF KNOWLEDGE

1986, Fifth month, Fascicule no: 17, Page 151

"The misunderstanding of the chapters in the book of Islam, introducing the jinn as EVIL beings, has caused the Islamic society to end up in this stat...e"

Yes, the reason why the jinn introduced themselves as the spirits and the aliens, hiding their real identity, is implicitly connotated in the above sentence.

Because the Quran states the jinn are *enemies* to humans and warns them to protect themselves and stay away from the jinn..

Unfortunately, many communities are ignorant and unaware of the reality of the jinn who are referred to as the "Satan" due to their capacity to fool and misguide the people away from religion and the Rasul of Allah (saw).

This is true to such extent that even religious clerics with an official religious title think the Satan is a different being from the jinn, despite the fact the Quran makes a clear statement concerning this.

The jinn who <u>deceive and misguide humans</u> in order to rule over them are the ones who are referred to as "satan" in the Quran, i.e. the evil ones. In other words, satan is a category within the jinn species referring specifically to those who lead humans astray by imposing false beliefs.

The proof of this is the following verse:

"And [mention] when We said to the angels, 'Prostrate to Adam,' and all but Iblis prostrated. He was of the jinn..."[44]

This verse also reveals very clearly that the jinn do not accept the superiority of the human consciousness.

Here are some interesting verses from the chapter Ya-Sin regarding the jinn with satanic qualities who are referred to as "Satan":

"O Children of Adam... Did I not enjoin upon you (inform you), that you not serve Satan (body/bodily and unconscious state of existence deprived of the knowledge of the reality; ego driven existence), for indeed, he (this state of unconsciousness) is to you a clear enemy?"[45]

"Indeed, he (Satan) has caused many of you to go astray! Did you not use your intellect?"[46]

As can be seen the Quran makes explicit warnings against the jinn with its many verses. As the most critical trait of the jinn is their inability to accept the existence of humans who are far more superior to them in many ways, they make use of every opportunity to possess humans and rule over them as they like.

---

[44] Quran 18:50
[45] Quran 36:60
[46] Quran 36:62

This trait in mentioned in the following verse:

"O community of jinn, you have truly possessed (misled from reality) the vast majority of mankind." [47]

Hence, as the verse makes clear, the majority of mankind, either consciously or unconsciously, have become victims to the wrong ideas imposed by the jinn and as a result have become possessed by them, falling far from the Rasul of Allah (saw) and the Quran.

For, as I have already underlined many times, the sole purpose of the jinn is to render invalid the religion of Islam and to invalidate the teachings of the Rasul of Allah (saw).

---

[47] Quran 6:128

26

THE SATANIC JINN AND THEIR DENIAL OF THE QURAN AND THE RASUL

As can be seen from their own words, the biggest deception of the jinn, who love to play the innocent, is their act of striving to help humanity in the guise of the loyal servants of Allah.

The fact is, the jinn claim the Quran is no longer valid, the recommended practices of the Rasul of Allah (saw) are no longer necessary, and suggest that people should stop engaging in such activity. Despite this, they still claim they are guiding the people to the right path.

Wherever you go in the world, you will see that the followers of the religion of Islam solemnly believe in the following principle: The principles of Islam and the teachings of Muhammad (saw) the final Rasul, are valid until doomsday and that there will be no other sacred book revealed after the Quran.

Whereas, according to the **jinn,** also known as the **aliens**, none of the sacred books, namely the TORAH, THE PSALMS OF DAVID, THE BIBLE and THE QURAN are no longer in effect and therefore **THE BOOK OF THE GOLDEN AGE** has come into effect. The jinn on the other hand are extremely benevolent beings who are willing to spend much effort to protect the human race and sacrifice everything they have in order to be of assistance to them. The jinn who are also called the **SATAN** are not actually bad beings at all, they are our valuable friends who inform the people of the obsoleteness of the Quran and the Rasul of Allah, the teachings of whom are for primitive human beings (!)

Let us see what the jinn say about this:

THE KNOWLEDGE BOOK OF THE GOLDEN AGE

Fascicule: 34, Page: 319

"Let us disclose the matter of the JINN and the SATAN to the public consciousness.

According to the MECHANISM OF THE RABB, the advanced levels of consciousness have been veiled in your sacred books so that terrestrial consciousness can attain the GODLY dimensions, and hence the advanced dimensions have been introduced to you inversely as the JINN and the DEVIL or SATAN... This is why your sacred books tell you to fear them and stay away from them, as the level of consciousness pertaining to that time period need not digress from the GODLY path."

Look at what the jinn, who present themselves as crucially benevolent beings under the guise of 'aliens' and who act like the saviors of humankind, say about religion, the Nabis and the Rasuls:

THE KNOWLEDGE BOOK OF THE GOLDEN AGE

Fascicule No: 41 – Page No: 390

"Let us repeat again. The time of RELIGIONS and PROPHETS is over. Now, you are the scientific projections of the Divine Dimension."

Meanwhile our alien friends do not accept that Muhammad is the Rasul of Allah (saw) and claim the following:

THE KNOWLEDGE BOOK OF THE GOLDEN AGE

Fascicule No: 42 – Page No: 408

"The Islamic Totality thinks that the enlightened friend MUHAMMAD is the RASUL. However, he is merely the messenger of the RASUL of ALLAH. The RASUL is the great ASHOT that is the GREAT PEACE."

According to the jinn who present themselves as the aliens and who are actually accepted as such by those who are not aware of the reality behind this phenomenon, **MOSES (pbuh), JESUS (pbuh), MUHAMMAD**

166

MUSTAFA (saw) and **MUSTAFA KEMAL** are all extraterrestrials, or the jinn, disguised as human beings.

Take a look at the message conveyed from the sacred BOOK OF KNOWLEDGE relating to this subject.

THE KNOWLEDGE BOOK OF THE GOLDEN AGE

Fascicule No: 24 – Page No: 216

"Missionaries for enlightenment were sent to you from these dimensions in the past. Let us convey them to you by their Terrestrial names: MOSES – JESUS CHRIST – MUHAMMAD MUSTAFA – MUSTAFA KEMAL. These are direct incarnations. In your own expression: They are direct extraterrestrials."

As a matter of fact, the jinn are not in favor of the idea of being called aliens or extraterrestrials, but they don't have much choice for if the fact that they are the jinn is known, no matter what they do, they will never be able to gain the trust of humans.

As can be seen from the statement above, after stating they are *of them*, they accept that "they are extraterrestrials" in *our words and expression!*

For them, being of the jinn is a matter of honor and pride. Due to their radial form free from the constrains of time and space their conditions of living are superior to ours. They can easily penetrate into the brains of mediums and psychics whose receptors are extremely sensitive and make them see extraordinary visions.

The fact that the teachings and the authority of the Quran, which was revealed by Muhammad (saw) the Rasul of Islam, is **valid until the doomsday** is a big problem for the jinn.

For, whenever they claim the Quran and Muhammad (saw) are *no longer valid* in these times, the Muslims counterclaim that the authorities and teachings of the Quran and Muhammad (saw) are absolutely valid until resurrection takes place.

So, in order to be able, continue asserting their delusive story the jinn have devised a new solution. They redefined the concept of doomsday and resurrection:

THE KNOWLEDGE BOOK OF THE GOLDEN AGE

Fascicule No: 25 – Page No: 222

"This FINAL AGE which is called the period of RESURRECTION in Your Sacred Books, is your planets' period of awakening and reaching higher consciousness. It is called the AGE OF MEDIUMS or the AGE OF CLAIRVOYANCE. During this period which is also called the period of SINCERITY and DEVOTION, the Celestial Authorities are validating the supremacy of humans both to themselves and to the universe by removing the intermediaries."

Yes, according to the jinn, the period of the doomsday has started long ago. Until 1999 mankind will suddenly awaken and the doomsday will thus take place. The signs of doomsday informed by Muhammad (saw) and the Quran will not occur, everything will transpire by the aid of cosmic effects (!)

Whether you accept them as the aliens or as the jinn, by whichever name you call them, the most prominent attribute of these beings is their ability to lead people astray using the concept of "god."

They present limitless gods and lords, and they exalt one over the other, and in their messages, they constantly use terms like Gods, Lords, Lordly Plans, and Godly Plans.

Here is an example:

THE KNOWLEDGE BOOK OF THE GOLDEN AGE

Fascicule No: 25 – Page No: 225

"The Book of Knowledge is bestowed on your planet from this system. The LORD OF THE WORLD is responsible for this. The LORD of the WORLD, AMON and RA are the direct projectors of the Plan as the ternary code. RA here is the LORD of the System. This is an operational order."

And all of these LORDS and GODS are all FEMALES. Here is the explanation pointing to this claim.

THE KNOWLEDGE BOOK OF THE GOLDEN AGE

Fascicule No: 34 – Page No: 319

"Everything is feminine in essence. In flesh and in action, it is masculine. Never forget this. All PROPHETS and even GODS are females."

Therefore, the prophet of this religion must also be a female. In fact, the 68 years old psychic lady who receives these so-called divine revelations is also a female.

Take a look at how the Quran warned against the jinn who claim the existence of female lords, 1400 years ago:

> **Those who turn to things other than Allah turn only to lifeless female deities in His stead, and hence they turn to none but the persistent malicious Satan (ego)!**
>
> **Allah has cursed (Iblis)... For Iblis had said, "I will surely take from among Your servants a significant portion"** ...
>
> **"And I will surely mislead them, and I will arouse in them** (sinful, bodily, empty) **desires, and I will command them so they slit the ears of cattle** (as sacrifice)**, and I will command them so they will alter the creation of Allah." And whoever deserts Allah and takes Satan** (bodily temptations; ego) **as master has certainly suffered a great loss.**
>
> **Satan promises them and arouses false hope and desire in them. But Satan does not promise anything except delusion.**[48]

---

[48] Quran 4 : 117 - 120

THE KNOWLEDGE BOOK OF THE GOLDEN AGE

Fascicule No: 10 – Page No: 86

"Each Galaxy has a LORD Mechanism. These LORDS are not the Absolute Almighty."

Indeed, the Lord of the world is different, the Lord of other planets is different, the Lord of the solar system is different, the Lord of the galaxy is different and the Lord of the all the other galaxies are all different from one another.

In short, there are unlimited number of female lords!

"Had there been within both (the heavens and the earth) gods besides Allah, surely this system would have lost its order. Allah, the Rabb of the Throne, is beyond the definitions they attribute to Him."[49]

Those who accept the Quran as a sacred book and confirm that Muhammed (saw) is the Rasul of Allah (saw) know well that the jinn are dangerous beings from whom one should stay away and protect himself.

For, the jinn, constantly give messages that render the religion of Islam invalid, through the assistance of mediums and psychics, in attempt to lead people away from religion. Because of this, the existence of the jinn is usually covered up by the jinn themselves.

Here's an example which points to this reality.

THE KNOWLEDGE BOOK OF THE GOLDEN AGE

Fascicule No: 10 – Page No: 86

'Fear is primitiveness; there is no Heaven, no Hell, no Jinn, no Fairy and no Devil. These are each the negative reflections of the conditioned consciousness'.

---

[49] Quran 21:22

Yes, on page 86 of this book it openly states there are no jinn. However, on pages 151 – 152 – 153 it also states that the aliens are actually the jinn. This is a typical example of the contradictory nature of the jinn.

So, is the Quran telling the truth or the jinn who present themselves as the aliens telling the truth?

According to the Quran, the teachings of Muhammad (saw), and the Islamic scholars and gnostics, the jinn who have satanic qualities and who are known as the 'Satan' are enemies to humans.

They spend their days striving to lead humans astray from religious truths, veil them from the reality of the life after death, weaken their belief in Allah, and encourage them to rebel against the commands of Allah, making them abandon the tenants of '*Amantu*' by imposing various confusing ideas onto them.

The jinn who present themselves as our guardians of supreme consciousness, consider it their duty to delude humans from the religion of Islam, and with this purpose they deny the Satan and claim the Satan is simply a power produced by the human mind.

So, what do the jinn with satanic qualities do? Of course, they carry out satanic acts!

First, they present themselves as the aliens, then they claim to be Allah, and then they reduce and simplify the meaning of Allah, eventually leading people to atheism.

According to the teachings of the Quran and Muhammad (saw), as the day of judgement draws near, just before the descent of Jesus (pbuh) onto the earth, about 30 false prophets will appear and declare that the present religions are no longer valid encouraging the people to accept the religion they present instead. Soon after this event takes place, the *Dajjal* (Antichrist) will appear and claim that he is the long awaited '**MESSIAH**' our savior!

This being referred to as the *Dajjal* will claim that the world is living its final days and that he is the Supreme Lord, further claiming that he is here to save those who believe in his commands and accept him as Allah the almighty. In order to prove this, claim he will manifest extraordinary events.

After the person with the *Mahdi* quality, who is aligned with the teachings of the Rasul of Allah (saw) and the Quran, communicates the message that the concept of 'ALLAH' is infinite, free from all limitations and that it is the very existence that comprises the universe, the *Dajjal* (Antichrist) will appear and literally put this teaching to the test by declaring the exact opposite.

He will claim to be 'ALLAH' and rule on earth for some time during which great masses of people around the world will believe in him and follow his path. It is openly stated in authentic *hadith* books by the Rasul of Allah (saw) that the *Dajjal* (Antichrist) will be killed by Jesus (pbuh) who will descend to the earth around the same time. This event is not open to interpretation and will manifest exactly as it is stated.

As a matter of fact, at this present time, the jinn disguised as the aliens are conveying the message that the **Supreme Lord** of mankind is going to descend to the earth with the army of the **LORD of the WORLD** and those who are under his command.

The concept of Allah that is explained in the religion of Islam and the Quran, specifically in the chapter al-Ikhlas, is something completely different to the concept of **GOD** described here.

Those who are interested may refer to **'Muhammad's Allah'** for further detail.

After enlightening us on the subject of Allah who is apparently embodied as a human, our alien friends claim that they also receive messages from Allah directly.

THE KNOWLEDGE BOOK OF THE GOLDEN AGE

Fascicule No: 46 - Page: 451

"Allah, whom you have known until today as The ONE is me. Yes, do not be surprised. At the moment, I, too, live in BETA NOVA in a body. The GRAND FATHER who lives on the UHUD Mountain at the Omega dimension projects my commands from that mountain to the universes, on cosmoses. (UHUD Mountain is a crystal mountain.) Each nucleic world

present in my system is the exact twin of the world you are in. In fact, the GRAND FATHER, too, lives in a nucleic world like this. Just like I live and await you in BETA NOVA at the moment. JESUS CHRIST is His son. However, the sexual reproduction here is imaginative, not physical.

He received his gene engraftment seed from Archangel GABRIEL.

The time has now come for us to talk like two friends.

The time has now come for me to inform the truth to those who wonder how I give messages to you. BETA NOVA is a green world, it is the (first main nucleus) of the BETA GURZ, which my human beings will form and live in.

I became EMBODIED HERE by transforming my energy with all my power into crude matter, in order to come here. I came in order to be with you.

And I will establish my fourth order here, in the just world nucleus... After I establish my order, I will leave my humanity order to my human beings within the GURZ and I will RETURN TO MY PLACE. As always, I can answer all your questions without any intermediaries. However, I can only unite with those who see the light of the consciousness of my conscious totality. This message of mine is for you and for the essences who comprehend me."

ALLAH "The One"

Look at the warnings made by the Quran against the jinn 1400 years ago:

"Yet they attributed the jinn (invisible beings) as partners onto Allah – while He (Allah) has created them (the qualities they manifest comprise Allah's Names)!"[50]

Apart from deceiving others, the jinn have no knowledge whatsoever on anything else and almost everything they do is in a backwards fashion, including their writings. According to the message conveyed in the sacred book sent by the aliens, the **Lord** of the world is a **jinn** whose name is **RANTIMUS.** When you read the word RAN backwards, you get the word NAR. This is a word which means 'fire' in Turkish. The Quran asserts that the jinn are created from fire. The planet that is referred by the name NAR

---

[50] Quran 6:100

here is the planet of fire. The jinn call this the dimension of OMEGA. It is a radial dimension. According to their claim, the name of their president in this dimension is called RANTIMUS which basically means the leader of that which is composed of fire.

Let us now take a look at how the **Dimension of Omega** is explained as the dimension which belongs to the **jinn.**

THE KNOWLEDGE BOOK OF THE GOLDEN AGE

Fascicule 47 / Page: 460

"We would like to disclose to you the word HARAN which is the supervising mechanism of the dimension of the truth. Each letter of this comprehensive word is a cipher code connected to the frequency of a word. However, at the same time, it also symbolizes the FIRE dimensions of the plains of truth. As you know the OMEGA dimension was also called the RAN planet. That is, the FIRE planet. The word fire utilized in this dimension expresses the powerful intensity of energies. However, RAN, that is NAR, is the blazing, flaming, shining fire. It has nothing to do with energy. HARAN is the power of fire of dimensions of truth."

As can be seen from here, the jinn, under the guise of aliens, openly confess that they belong to a structure that is made of fire.

LEST YOU ARE DECEIVED!

Indeed, the most prominent activity and business of the "aliens" is to delude, frighten, and induce false hope to humans, taking them under their possession by making them believe they are "the chosen ones."

Yes, the jinn, who sometimes introduce themselves as the Satan and demons - but then claim to be "benevolent' beings in essence - and at other times entertain us by claiming to be our celestial savors, take great delight in flattering humans by making them believe they are "the chosen ones"!

Take a look at how the Quran warns against this bait:

> **Except Iblis; he** (relying on his mind) **was arrogant and became of those who deny the knowledge of the reality** (those who cannot recognize the essential reality of others due to their egos)[51]

> **And [mention] when We said to the angels, 'Prostrate to Adam,' and all but Iblis prostrated. He was of the jinn...**[52]

When the being (from the jinn species) who used to be called "Azazil" in the past was asked to prostrate to humans he fell into a dichotomy and was hence called "Iblis"! And after this refusal to prostrate, when he decided to lead humans astray, i.e. manifest his satanic attributes, he was

---

[51] Quran 38:74
[52] Quran 18:50

called the Satan. It was after this that the jinn were called demons, because the jinn started to attack mankind with their satanic attributes.

Look at how the Quran warns against the jinn who are referenced by the word "Satan":

> **A group of you He guided and a group deserved to be in falsity! Indeed, they** (those who went astray) **had taken the devils** (the deviators) **as allies instead of Allah, and they consider themselves as rightly guided!**[53]

> (Lot) **said, "My Rabb, help me against these corrupting people!"**[54]

> **Thereupon Satan whispered suspicions to them to make them aware of their ego and corporeality...** [55]

> **And he swore to them, 'Indeed, I am from among the advisors'**[56]

> **O Children of Adam... Did I not enjoin upon you** (inform you), **that you not serve Satan** (body/bodily and unconscious state of existence deprived of the knowledge of the reality; ego driven existence), **for indeed, he** (this state of unconsciousness) **is to you a clear enemy?**[57]

> **Satan** (corporeality; the idea of being just the physical body) **has overcome them and made them forget the remembrance of Allah** (their own reality of which they have been reminded, and that they will abandon their bodies and live eternally as 'consciousness' comprised of Allah's Names!) **Those** (who are receptive to satanic impulses and think of themselves as only the physical body) **are the acquaintances of Satan. Take heed, most assuredly, the partisans of Satan are the very losers!**[58]

---

[53] Quran 7:30
[54] Quran 29:38
[55] Quran 7:20
[56] Quran 7:21
[57] Quran 36:60
[58] Quran 58:19

And whoever is blinded (with external things) **from the remembrance of *Rahman*** (remembering that his essential reality is composed of the names of Allah and thus from living the requirements of this)**, We appoint for him a Satan** (a delusion; the idea that he is only the physical body and that life should be lived in pursuit of bodily pleasures) **and this** (belief) **will become his** (new)**identity! And indeed, these will avert them from the way** (of the reality) **while they think they are on the right path!**[59]

Indeed, Iblis proved his assumption (regarding man) **to be correct, except for some of the believers, they all followed him. And yet he** (Iblis) **had no influential power over them at all! We only did this to reveal who really believes in their eternal life to come and who is in doubt thereof. Your Rabb is *Hafiz* over all things.**[60]

As can be seen, the jinn with satanic qualities are constantly doing everything they possibly can to lead people away from religion.

In order to veil their true face and nature, they constantly appear under different names and in different forms, creating gods and lords in universes beyond imagination to amuse and delude the masses.

Unfortunately, they have possessed an unimaginable number of people on earth today…

Let us remember and take heed of the following verse:

"O community of jinn, you have truly possessed (misled from reality) the vast majority of mankind."

The serious and extensive warnings made in the Quran against the jinn who possess humans under the guise of various names and forms are of paramount importance for the thinking brain!

---

[59] Quran 43: 36-37
[60] Quran 34: 20-21

28

HOW CAN WE PROTECT OURSELVES?

I have provided extensive information on this in *The Power of Prayer*...

Additionally...

The jinn, according to the teachings of the Quran, caused great suffering to Job (pbuh) who saved himself by continually reciting the prayer I will share below.

The waves produced and emitted by the brain as a result of repeating this prayer not only forms a protective magnetic shield around one's brain, but also renders the jinn ineffective, much like the mosquito repellant tablets that neutralize and repel mosquitos - the jinn are left powerless and forced to move away.

Reciting the chapters 'Al-Falaq', 'An-Nas' and 'Ayat al-Qursi' from the Quran strengthen the spirit, enabling the person to resist and oppose the jinn.

The prayer below however, is composed of various verses from the Quran and acts very much like the beams of a laser gun that directly shoot at the jinn forcing them to escape.

If you recite this prayer silently near those who believe in the "aliens" you will see that their jinn will make them get up and leave that place. Or, they will begin to sweat and feel distressed and lose their ability to articulate, mumbling things that don't really make sense.

In order to set free one who is under such intense influence at least a few people need to come together and collectively read this prayer to the person, whereby each person recites it 300 times within the same time frame and with the same intention. In fact, they should repeat this three times every other day.

If the person reads this prayer on himself, without support from others, he will begin to feel agitated after repeating it 30-50 times, his body temperature will begin to rise and he will feel immensely tired and eventually fall asleep. This is because he is under the influence of the jinn who are sending impulses to his brain to stop him from reciting the prayer. If the person resists and continues to recite, eventually these effects will begin to subside and the person will feel relieved. But in any case, it is highly recommended that he continues reciting this prayer for at least a month.

On the other hand, no matter how many times it is recited by those who are not possessed by the jinn, none of the symptoms mentioned above will be seen.

So let me make my final warning on this subject. In order to protect oneself from the jinn, one must acquire knowledge on them. Let us then acquire proper knowledge, apply the formulas and warn those around us so that they too can protect themselves.

THE PRAYERS FOR PROTECTION

Rabbi annee massani ash-shaytaanu binuṣubin wa `adhaabin rabbi a`oodhu bika min hamazaati ash-shaytaani wa a`oodhu bika rabbi an yaḥḍurooni wa ḥifẓan min kulli shaytaanin maaridin.[61]

Meaning:

My Rabb (The reality of the Names comprising my essence)! **Satan** (the internal mechanism (ego) that promotes the illusory existence of the inexistent and veils the Absolute Reality) **is distressing and tormenting me. My Rabb, I seek refuge in You from the incitements of Satan, and I seek refuge in You from the presence of Satanic influences**

---

[61] Quran 38:41, 23:97-98, 37:07

around me. And You have provided protection from every rebellious Satan.

A`aoodhu bi wajhi l-llahil kareem wa kalimaati l-ta'ammatillati la yujaawiz huna barun wa la fa'ajirun min sharri maa yanzilu mina s-samaa-i wa maa y`aruju feeha wa min sharri maa dhara fee-l ardhi wa mayakhrujoo minha wa min fitanil layli wan nahari wa min sharri kulli taariqin illa tariqan yatruku bikhayrin ya Rahman.

Meaning:

I seek refuge in the countenance of Allah, the Kareem (the exceedingly generous and bountiful), and in all of His Names, nothing good or bad can attack them. I seek refuge in RAHMAN from that which ascends to the heavens (provocative illusory thoughts) and that which descends from the heavens (thoughts that conjure doubt and suspicion), from that which is produced from the earth (that which emanates from corporeality) and grows out of it (bodily demands and desires), from the provocations of the day (our internal life) and the night (the outside world), and from that which knocks on the door at night (instinct), except with good.

29

CONCLUDING THOUGHTS

Muhyiddin Ibn Arabi was declared an infidel and an unbeliever by narrow minded people who were far from reaching his level. They wanted to banish him simply because he was sharing truths that could not be attained by everyone.

A man named "Galileo" emerged in the West and claimed the "Earth spins" for which he was charged with heresy and faced Inquisition! He was accused of being irreligious, he was called a deviant, and they wanted to execute him! He too was harshly prone to the wrath of bigotry of his time simply because he wanted to share truths that were not easily attainable by everyone.

There is a common cause in both scenarios. The denial of those who are unaware of their incognizance and their tendency to discard truths which they can't reach, as non-existent.

Similar scenarios have taken place endless times throughout the centuries…

Such individuals disclose a reality to the people, those who care to listen attempt to evaluate it according to their own level of understanding and the result is always the same: denial!

However, there is also another reality. Time always proves them right!

Whether it be 10, 50 or 100 years later, at some point or another mankind comes around to accepting the truth they presented and end up having to follow the path that they have shown. For, those who follow other paths eventually and inevitably come to a dead-end whereby they have to turn back…

History shows us time and time again, those who present an idea to the world for the first time have always been criticized, ridiculed and subject to insulting behavior.

Even the Rasul (saw) of humanity was slandered and accused of being a crazy sorcerer…

Thus, it is evident that one who offers a gift to mankind is always faced with heavy reactions at the onset. Because what they offer goes against the conventional truth; it is outside the scope of what people know and are accustomed to.

So, I have put together this book after enduring research and extensive study… and included many new ideas and truths for the first time in the world.

This book presents unique information on the following subjects:

1. The attributes of the SPIRIT,

2. The make-up and qualities of MAN,

3. The make-up and characteristics of the JINN,

4. The inner truth of SPIRITISM.

If read with care it will be seen that none of the information is contrary to logic and science. There isn't a single point that contradicts religious teachings either.

After I completed the book, I realized the emphasis weighed heavier on the subject of the jinn.

This is because, for the first time in the world, I have provided interpretations on two verses of the Quran in the light of science.

The fact that spiritism and the concept of aliens have become so widespread, to the point that it is almost recognized as a new religion, has led me to cover this topic in more detail.

I'm assuming a book on the jinn with such comprehensive and scientific explanations has not been written before. This being said, I'm not as naive as to claim superiority over anyone!

If a book on the jinn has not been written until today, then this should not be attributed to the ignorance of the people who lived in the past but rather to the inadequacy of scientific resources of their time…

There is no doubt that many who have lived in the past knew about these realities before me, however the insufficiency of scientific knowledge didn't allow them to explain it at the level that I am able to today…

As for my thoughts regarding humans… once these ideas are examined carefully it will be seen that they are in fact very logical. Sooner or later science will verify my claims. Religion has already validated these truths 1400 years ago… All my claims are completely aligned with the teachings of religion.

I did not place too much emphasis on the subject of humans since I have already done that in *"The Human Enigma"* … But since this topic is closely related to the subject of spirits, jinn and spiritism, I made some reference to humans, in particular the material make-up of the human body.

With regard to the subject of the SPIRIT, it is impossible to know what it is in its *entirety*. However, this does not mean that humans are completely incapable of attaining some of its truths.

I agree with the great Islamic Sufi master *Ismail Hakkı Bursevi,* who asserts that everybody could attain some knowledge on the nature of the **'SPIRIT'** with respect to their capacity. I believe that this is the meaning referenced by the relevant verses in the Quran.

However, I can easily tell you that **'SPIRITISM'** is nothing other than invoking the jinn, i.e. what used to be known as the **'Science of Huddam'** in the past, and with which humanity has been familiar since the time of Moses (pbuh). I assert this with comfort because science is on our side now allowing us to express these truths with more confidence.

I'm hoping that after this book is published, all the Muslims will be able to accept and confess the existence of the jinn with more ease and without the fear of being labelled or accused of 'being superstitious.

As a matter of fact, it is becoming more and more apparent that it is indeed those who reject the existence of the jinn themselves who are narrowminded and unscientific.

To conclude…

I am presenting unique ideas and concepts in this book that have never been shared before.

Sooner or later, humanity will accept these ideas and find it necessary to pursue their pointing to attain results which have not been imagined of until now.

On the other hand, there will always be those who refuse to accept these ideas and deny them simply because it goes against their vested interests!

I accept all of these probabilities at the onset and present my work with the comfort and the great pleasure of sharing exclusive and valuable knowledge with mankind…

I have no doubt that the facts I'm stating in this book for the first time in the world will sooner or later be evaluated in a way that they deserve. Even if I'm not able to see this!

AHMED HULUSI
21 December 1971
Cerrahpasa
ISTANBUL

ABOUT THE AUTHOR

Ahmed Hulusi (Born January 21, 1945, Istanbul, Turkey) contemporary Islamic philosopher. From 1965 to this day he has written close to 30 books. His books are written based on Sufi wisdom and explain Islam through scientific principles. His established belief that the knowledge of Allah can only be properly shared without any expectation of return has led him to offer all of his works which include books, articles, and videos free of charge via his web-site. In 1970 he started examining the art of spirit evocation and linked these subjects parallel references in the Quran (smokeless flames and flames instilling pores). He found that these references were in fact pointing to luminous energy which led him to write *Spirit, Man, Jinn* while working as a journalist for the Aksam newspaper in Turkey. Published in 1985, his work called *The Human Enigma (Insan ve Sirlari)* was Hulusi's first foray into decoding the messages of the Quran filled with metaphors and examples through a scientific backdrop. In 1991 he published *The Power of Prayer (Dua and Zikir)* where he explains how the repetition of certain prayers and words can lead to the realization of the divine attributes inherent within our essence through increased brain capacity. In 2009 he completed his final work, '*Decoding the Quran, A Unique Sufi Interpretation*' which encompasses the understanding of leading Sufi scholars such as Abdulkarim al Jili, Abdul-Qadir Jilani, Muhyiddin Ibn al-Arabi, Imam Rabbani, Ahmed ar-Rifai, Imam Ghazali, and Razi, and which approached the messages of the Quran through the secret Key of the letter 'B'.

NOTES

Printed in Great Britain
by Amazon

81951276R00120